Olympic Ceremonialism and the Performance of
National Character

DOI: 10.1057/9781137336323

Other Palgrave Pivot titles

DOI: 10.1057/9781137336323

palgrave▸pivot

Olympic Ceremonialism and The Performance of National Character: From London 2012 to Rio 2016

Rodanthi Tzanelli
University of Leeds, UK

palgrave
macmillan

DOI: 10.1057/9781137336323

First published 2013 by
PALGRAVE MACMILLAN

Palgrave Macmillan in the UK is an imprint of Macmillan Publishers Limited, registered in England, company number 785998, of Houndmills, Basingstoke, Hampshire RG21 6XS.

Palgrave Macmillan in the US is a division of St Martin's Press LLC, 175 Fifth Avenue, New York, NY 10010.

Palgrave Macmillan is the global academic imprint of the above companies and has companies and representatives throughout the world.

Palgrave® and Macmillan® are registered trademarks in the United States, the United Kingdom, Europe and other countries.

ISBN: 978-1-137-33633-0 EPUB
ISBN: 978-1-137-33632-3 PDF
ISBN: 978-1-137-33631-6 Hardback

A catalogue record for this book is available from the British Library.

A catalog record for this book is available from the Library of Congress.

www.palgrave.com/pivot

DOI: 10.1057/9781137336323

For Majid, as always
In memory of my grandfather, who worked as a boat mechanic and
never liked holidays

DOI: 10.1057/9781137336323

Contents

DOI: 10.1057/9781137336323

DOI: 10.1057/9781137336323

List of Figures

DOI: 10.1057/9781137336323

Acknowledgements

This book represents the end of an unlikely journey that commenced during fieldwork I conducted for a British Academy project 'Reciprocal Orientalisms: Understanding Thessaloniki's Ottoman Past through Multiple Narrations' (2009–11). The term 'conduct' is appropriate, as the project's theoretical musings were informed by an urgency to understand the role of culturally specific *rhythms* in a world constantly defying cultural borders raised by national memory. My transition from investigations into poverty, segregation and artistic exclusivity to an analysis of artistic performance in more privileged socio-cultural contexts does not produce a cacophony or a 'musical dissonance', so to speak. It is a sociological exercise with its own merits, including an attempt to analyse creativity with an eye to context. In 2012, Britain faces possibly one of the worst economic crises and expenditure on public extravaganzas such as those of the Olympic Games can only provoke criticism. But social developments in all spheres of human activity, including art*work* (or *art*work) deserve consideration in their own right as much as they stand as symbolic manifestations of the turmoil in which they are born. Here I only provide one perspective on this endless debate, prompting readers to consider the book an introduction to those 'epistemologies of silence', rumour and whisper any work of art is bound to produce. My own analytical and normative volume is kept deliberately very low so as to blend better.

I am grateful to Andrew James and Naomi Campbell from Palgrave Macmillan for their help with the production of the book. Thanks to Eleni Theodoraki and Louise Todd for sharing their PowerPoint presentation on Olympic brands and the members of the TRINET digital network who responded to my calls for help for bibliography on samba and tourism. I am also grateful to Vassos Argyrou for allowing me to cite from the manuscript of his forthcoming book *The Gift of European Thought and the Cost of Living* (Berghahn, 2013) and my PhD student, John Poulter, who was happy to share his knowledge on British and Irish memory work in television. I am grateful to Rob Fuller and EZTD Photography/BBC for allowing me to use two of his spectacular images (Figures 3.1 and 3.2). Thanks also to Andrew Osborne for letting me use his great photo from the Rio handover ceremony (Figure 4.1), Sam Harvey for his professional photo of the ArchelorMittal Orbit (Figure 2.6), Shimelle Laine for the images of the Industrial Revolution and the Olympic Rings (Figures 2.2, 2.3 and 2.4) and Elizabeth Harkin for the photos of the Olympic Cauldron and the Bell (Figures 2.1 and 2.5). The extended Wikipedia articles on the London 2012 Opening and Closing Ceremonies served as guides to the press coverage of the events. Aspects of Chapter 1 were inspired by the following articles: R. Tzanelli (2012) 'The Greek Fall: Simulacral thanatotourism in Europe', *The Global Studies Journal*, 5(1), 105–20; R. Tzanelli (2010) 'Mediating cosmopolitanism: Crafting an allegorical imperative through Beijing 2008', *International Review of Sociology*, 20(2), 215–41; and R. Tzanelli (2008) 'The nation has two voices: *Diforia* and performativity in Athens 2004', *European Journal of Cultural Studies*, 11(4), 489–508. Neither article figures in the book in its original form.

DOI: 10.1057/9781137336323

List of Abbreviations

GOSH	Great Ormond Street Hospital
IAAF	International Association of Athletics Federation
IFFHS	International Federation of Football History & Statistics
IOC	International Olympic Committee
LOCOG	London (2012) Organising Committee for the Olympic Games
LSO	London Symphony Orchestra
NHS	National Health Service
ROCOG	Rio (2016) Organising Committee for the Olympic Games

Note on the Author

Dr Rodanthi Tzanelli is lecturer in sociology at the University of Leeds, UK. She is author of over 60 articles and six monographs, including *Cosmopolitan Memory in Europe's Backwaters: Rethinking Civility* (2011), and *Heritage in the Digital Era: Cinematic Tourism and the Activist Cause* (2013).

▶

DOI: 10.1057/9781137336323

1
The Olympic Industry: Slow and Fast Mobilities

Abstract: *This chapter argues that Olympic ceremonies are situated between slow and fast mobilities – or, national histories and the history and principles of Olympism on the one hand, and ideas of travel and tourism on the other. This is developed through foundational concepts in tourism theory, such as that of tórnos that allows for connections between work/labour and leisure in Olympic industries in general and ceremonies in particular. The model of the tornadóros is used to analyse how ceremonial directors and Olympic artists use various digital, audio-visual and embodied technologies to communicate with audiences. These artistic tornadóroi are compared with athletes, who are supposed to conform to special types of 'human' that promote the principles of Olympism.*

Tzanelli, Rodanthi. *Olympic Ceremonialism and The Performance of National Character: From London 2012 to Rio 2016.* Basingstoke: Palgrave Macmillan, 2013. DOI: 10.1057/9781137336323.

1.1   Introducing the project

Since their modern institution, the Olympic Games experienced a number of structural transformations in their delivery, performance and political concerns. Encoding national, regional and cosmopolitan concerns about the political development of host cities (e.g. their cultural beautification, tourist growth or global projection of multi-cultural aspirations), the post-war summer Olympiads also acted as narratives of national agendas. The opening and closing ceremonies in particular frame the event, constructing one of the 'public faces' of the host in the event (De Moragas et al., 2002). As mediatised images of ethno-cultural essence gained more in global circulation, marketability and malleability, ceremonial Olympism began to place more emphasis on the host's self-presentation. The present book examines the London 2012 opening and closing ceremonies as artistic sources of national and cosmopolitan belonging. Looking at connections and disconnections of Olympic images from their production contexts, the project builds on Appadurai's (1990) thesis on interconnected 'scapes' or symbolic meeting points of humans, ideas, technologies, finance and images.

The synergy of embodied performances with projected simulations on big flat screens in the stadium produced an 'artscape' (Tzanelli, 2012a, p. 284), a technological transposition of emotive landscapes and a visualisation of material cultures. 'Art' is understood here as a by-product of communicative democratisation – the craft of communication (the material of everyday life) and its high aesthetics (as in fine arts). There is a cautionary note attached to such democratisations in so far as artistic performance always strives for concrete definitions of popular commonality (see for example Couldry, 2006; Hesmondhalgh, 2007a). The ceremonies draw upon the athletic ideas of embodied wellbeing and unrestrained flourishing but also the – yet unresolved – debate on national and cosmopolitan belonging that guides the production of individual Games and the International Olympic Committee's (IOC) ethical agendas. The adjacent development of the Olympic Games into consumption nodes, in which host cities operate as 'global financial articulations' (Sassen, 2001; Urry, 2008), connects the book's thesis to the commercialisation of the arts. I therefore treat London 2012's art system as an example of new mobilities (of ideas, art, images, music and more).

Research on such ceremonies often emphasises the organisational and institutional aspects of mega-events such as the Olympic Games.

DOI: 10.1057/9781137336323

However, this sheds more light on media policies, as well as the politics of the Olympic creative industries. Such processes would naturally link back to the creative labour that supports Olympic mega-events and which is constitutive of global human flows (Caves, 2002; Hesmondhalgh, 2007b). The present monograph only touches upon this debate to acknowledge the disorganised collaboration of state agents, Olympic institutions and capitalist networks that partake in the organisation of the event (see Lash and Urry, 1987, chapter 1 on 'disorganised capitalism'). Placing more emphasis on the content and cultural context of the opening and closing ceremonies of the London 2012 Olympiad, the artistic directors and participants' biographies and their relation to the host's urban profile, it discusses how the ceremonies actualise utopian travels for the benefit of native and global audiences. Given the cosmopolitan makeup of these shows, I also provide some observations on the handover ceremony for Rio 2016 in a separate chapter. However, I do not want to reduce such intangible and tangible artistic products to specific individual actors' intentions or their social positions and identities (see however Garnham, 1990 on negotiations of power in cultural industries). Although such a stance illuminates the universalisation of value claims in any polity, I recognise that societies preserve a vastly complex network of values that pluralise understandings of taste but proceed to argue against the reduction of aesthetic judgement to ideologies hooked exclusively on social variables. Thus, my focus is on the ways artistic narratives acquire the value of national and cosmopolitan self-narration in a context which is defined by post-national abstractions based on intersectionality and dialogical positioning (for other analyses see Hogan, 2003; Silk, 2001; Tomlinson, 1996; Tomlinson, 2005; Tomlinson and Young, 2006; Tzanelli, 2008b and 2010a).

I mobilise a selection of instances from the three ceremonies to examine the ways nations are placed in a global realm of 'travelling cultures' in which fixities of custom and character are performed for global viewers. The British instance is noteworthy for more than one reason: not only has the country been the genetic locus of the Industrial Revolution, it also provided a post-industrial model of creativity for cultural industries globally. I am not interested in examining how the post-industrial mode defines those industries' political economy in structural terms – this is a theme in its own right. Instead, I look at the ways this novel model of artistic creativity incorporates ideas of imaginative travel and turns tourism into a marketing tool. As various scholars have suggested, unlike the

DOI: 10.1057/9781137336323

film industry, it is rather difficult to define tourism as a uniform industry (Cohen, 1996, p. 59; Lew, 2011; MacCannell, 2012, p. 184). The 'heterogeny and disarticulation' characterising it resembles the structure of other multi-industrial conglomerates that constantly expand into new areas (Hesmondhalgh, 2007b; Tzanelli, [2007] 2010b). My project examines global projections and embodied performances of the 'British economy of thought' in a ceremonial context. I argue that the idea of 'Britishness' crafted by various creative agents (directors, volunteers, actors) retained a revisionist feel we encounter in post-modern travelling cultures.

This 'economy of thought', to which I refer throughout the book, dates back to the demise of pre-industrial 'pure' reciprocities within and between human communities (Mauss, 1954; Sahlins, 1972). The onset of industrial modernity replaced such allegedly disinterested acts of giving with economic transactions (Polanyi, 1944). This model found an extension in intercultural and international relations in Europe and elsewhere, suggesting that whole groups owe to other groups historical debts (see Tzanelli, 2008a; Argyrou, 2013, forthcoming). The timeline of such debts has been documented by social theory, which tends to historicise the present in order to produce utopian imaginaries of humanity (Hviid Jacobsen and Tester, 2012, pp. 1–2). The industrialisation of the globe, which was based on travel and discovery, is a turning point in the globalised European economy of giving. I contend that Olympic ceremonies treat giving, travel and industry as a unity and a globalised 'civilising process' in which scholars and other analysts see the corruption of nature *and* human nature (Argyrou, 2005). The handover to Rio paralleled London's ceremonial motif while drawing nevertheless upon local or regional cultural registers impossible to be decoded by outsiders in their specificity but accessible as tourist narratives. Such 'travelling cultures' (Clifford, 1992) – mobile ideas of industry, reciprocity and travel – are both idealisations of fixities (of ethnic character) and programmatic statements of mobility and fluidity (Bauman, 2000; Urry, 2008). The ideal of crafting national characters in motion involves a great deal of embodied and digital manipulation. Rather than introvert versions of collective selves, these models are co-produced through London's and Britain's (as well as Rio's and Brazil's) encounters with the world. Their creators and audiences actualised a model of tourism and post-tourism on which I elaborate through tourism, art and social theory.

Recent research has taken great strides to move away from the cult of methodological nationalism that views the nation-state as pivotal in

DOI: 10.1057/9781137336323

productions and manipulations of identity (Beck, 2005; Sassen, 2006; Walby, 2009; Bailey and Winchester, 2012). Understandably, an analysis of the structural conditions under which any Olympic ceremony is authorised on behalf of a host city cannot avoid the vocabulary of nation-building altogether. As Bauman (1987) reminds us, we need to investigate who actually acts as an interpreter in such cultural conjunctions. It goes without saying that the Olympic Games operate as part of a globalised economy, connecting various cultural flows that look outside the national domain or 'ideology' (Giddens, 1985; Sampson and Bloor, 2007). But the globalisation of what I term an 'Olympic industry' is a topic of specialised concern and merits separate consideration. Suffice it to mention that my understanding of the 'Olympic industry' refers to a cultural industrial multiplex bound by constellations of 'signs' whose meaning is delimited by various Olympic actors (sponsors, TV networks, music and other companies) (Tzanelli, [2007b] 2010b, Chapter 1). Any definition of the 'Olympic industry' follows a similar pattern: modern economies are consumption based, and 'social technologies that manage consumption derive from the social and creative disciplines' (Cunningham, 2005, p. 293; see also Billings, 2008). The present book is more concerned with global ideational formations propagated by artistic agents of the Olympic spectacle – otherwise put, ideals we cannot reduce to concrete human situations that nevertheless serve as the practical base for them. Not only do such formations envelop national fixities in global cultural mobilities, they also lead to their dilution. Elsewhere (Tzanelli, 2010a) I suggested that, in Olympic ceremonies, national self-narration takes place simultaneously in different expressive/visual modes, enabling the co-existence (and communication) of the 'symbolic' with the 'material', in what I termed the 'allegorical imperative'. This imperative, a miniature of the Olympic discourse on human dignity, is constitutive of the anthropopoetic project, the making of human.

1.2 Allegorical and categorical imperatives in Olympic art

We will follow this trend for a while, as it will lead us to the next important connection – namely that the ideal type of human crafted in ceremonies is cinematic-like fiction. This fiction centres on narratives of a being in motion we encounter in discourses of cosmopolitan travel and tourism.

DOI: 10.1057/9781137336323

The very philosophical trajectory of the concept of 'cosmopolitanism' bears testimony to this theoretical convergence: from Kant to Rousseau and from Durkheim to Meinecke, any 'cosmopolitan' respect for human diversity that promotes solidarity on a global scale is viewed as a condition that cannot be achieved solely through formalised agreement, as it also demands the development of moral sensitivity for specific cultural contexts (Tzanelli 2008b, p. 195). Should we then consider 'Olympic art' as the maiden of the nation-state, the moral guardian of cultural specificity? My own answer seeks to unveil a complexity that does not allow us to provide simple, affirmative answers. Every Olympic event enacts a tension between localised (national) self-knowledge and its universal application, actualising what is known as a 'diatopical hermeneutics' of difference based on processes of reciprocal learning in cross-cultural encounters (Dallmayr, 2001, p. 61). This simply refers to interpretations of human specificity in context, or, as the term denotes through (*diá*) place (*tópos*). One group of scholars would argue that place is defined by those who inhabit and control it – nations and nation-states. The equation of the individual with the national is as old as Herder's deliberation on the socio-cultural formation of our humanity and its linguistic articulation – a point guiding his suggestion that every national *Geist* (spirit) has unique, human-like, qualities and a special mission to carry out in the world (Bhatt, 2000). Just like humans, nations are unique; and just like them, they can be further abstracted by governors who want to regulate them.

I explained that today nations have given way to global flows. However, the ontological confusion of humans as individuals with nations as collectivities finds artistic expression in Olympic events for a global audience through certain universal motifs that 'sketch' an agreeable European/Hellenic civilisational model, the locus of 'high culture' (Jenks, 1993, p. 9), but apply native touches to it (Eagleton. 2000, p. 32). On initial consideration this recycled drama seems to mirror the Aristotelian *polítis* (the citizen of *pólis*) that Kant coupled with a socially constructed *kósmos* to produce an abstraction of the cosmopolitan subject (Delanty, 2006). But a literal meaning of *kósmos* (from *kosmó*: to make beautiful) introduces an aesthetic (cultural) dimension to it. Pedagogy, aesthetics and politics converge now behind the concept to suggest a method of 'knowing' through visual enactment and bodily performance. This model of cosmopolitan aesthetics, which informs the Olympic cultural enterprise, selectively borrows from the Kantian *sensus*

DOI: 10.1057/9781137336323

communis, the moral universe of human solidarity and togetherness, and the literal meaning of *kosmopolítis* as the subject that inhabits the space of the aesthetic (Delanty, 2000, p. 134). On the one hand, the model promotes the host to an 'aesthetically reflexive' (Beck, 1992; Beck et al., 1994; Lash and Urry, 1994, pp. 5–6) agent that monitors the social world rather than accepting a pre-determined place in it. The Olympic staging of national self-narration packages the host's heritage and history, creating long-lasting brands of emotional appeal, and integrating a culturally specific milieu into a global one (Albrow et al., 1997, pp. 30–1; Lury, 2004; Tzanelli, 2007b, pp. 77–81). On the other hand, the hosts' obstinate investment in a struggle to appropriate the European-Olympic heritage unveils the essence and function of the ceremonies as a reproduction of what they set out to contest (Guttman, 2006, pp. 72–3).

Kirshenblatt-Gimblett (1998) uses the term 'display interface' to analyse the context of performance through its mediation, detachment and re-contextualisation as 'heritage' for the tourist gaze. I argue that Olympic ceremonial mobilities capitalise on the aesthetic repositories of sport heritage and global tourism. First of all, the Kantian 'categorical imperative' (*Moralität*) that guides the IOC's discursive mantra of universal morality (togetherness, peace, fair play and athletic excellence) also informs the host's allegorical imperative (of excellent delivery, efficiency, and an impeccable public image built at the expense of internal difference) (Wilson, 1996). Category and allegory become good friends and bad enemies in Olympic events, when and if the need arises so as Olympic artists can produce a uniform style for the ceremonies of specific Games. I do not prioritise such artistic styles as a way of thinking at the expense of their organisational, if not institutional, aspects (Tomlinson and Young, 2006, p. 3). However, in the stead of an analysis of the institutional production of style (the emergence of a capitalist 'node' for every Summer Olympiad) I examine the modes of collective knowledge the ceremonial Olympiad voices (Becker, 1982; DeNora, 2000). I also do not confuse aesthetics with art and artistic style: my leap from aesthetics to artistic style suggests a socio-political reading of sensory experience and expression. With an eye to Mannheimian readings of 'artistic volition' (Mannheim, 2003), I view the modes of collective being and their artistic expression in relation to dominant views of the social world – the patterns of knowledge that find expression through styles (Mannheim, 1968 [1936], pp. 292–309; Witkin, 2005; de la Fuente, 2007, p. 413).

DOI: 10.1057/9781137336323

Of course, imperatives change with time and through human agency. This is more evident in today's art that can be post-national and post-modern (see Delanty, 2000, chapter 1). Nations as political and cultural formations are here to stay, so I cannot ignore their territorial and semantic claims over history and heritage altogether. At the same time, the present study focuses on the dialogic game artists play with fixities, hooking and unhooking them from the storerooms of national experience. In this respect, the host's allegorical imperative may be articulated in Olympic art loosely through successive re-encounters with rooted histories whose meaning – hence interpretations – is never exhausted (on Bloch and music see Born and Hesmondhalgh, 2000, p. 47 and p. 58 [ftn. p. 124]).The aesthetic genre of the Olympic ceremonies, the host's allegorical imperative, suggests that nation-building is an interpretive process just as art remains a socially informed process (Schechner, 1988; DeNora, 2003). Inversely, master narratives of culture with global applicability are constantly relocated in the national domain, generating new cultural grammars or reinstating the old European economy of thought (Honneth, 1992, p. 119). Markedly, 'Allegory' comprised the section of the Athens 2004 opening ceremony that mourned the burden Hellenic heritage creates for modern Greece and the country's inability to break free from this 'scarce resource' (Appadurai, 1981) of historical origins. Here unique narratives join global art markets as 'allegories', challenging old ideas of reciprocity, as they enter give-and-take economic circuits.

Allegories are community orations (*agorévō* from *agorá* as the ancient market) that take place elsewhere (*alloú*), public speech with private meaning through intercultural encounters that support creative ventures in arts. This model of allegory as performative expression follows other similar arguments and concepts that tie the production of identities and subjectivities to place, space and culture. In a similar vein with Foucault's heterotopias (*héteron*: other, *tópos*: place) allegories involve intentional misplacement of time-levels, enabling human actors to re-arrange experience and re-conceptualise phenomena (Foucault, 1986, pp. 16–17). Allegories can also be conceptualised as a form of *di-* or *multi-foría* (double- or poly-transference), twin or multiple ambivalence in identity. This phenomenon assists in performative enunciations of identity followed by slippage in meaning across different interpretive plains. Elsewhere, I examined the interpretative potential of ceremonies in terms of *diforia* as the activation of the performative aspects of national identity, 'resulting in a separation of the private (internal) and public (external)

DOI: 10.1057/9781137336323

worlds' (Tzanelli, 2008b, p. 491). Sport globalisation research would also propel us to see in Olympic allegories a process of 'arrogation' whereby national values 'are inevitably reshaped while being claimed as preserved' (Tomlinson, 1996, p. 590). Hence, I suggest that in Olympic art we experience a peculiar co-existence of mobility and immobility for good reasons: in modern and post-modern theory, mobility and any idea of a world-in-process (the grand narrative of modernity Olympic Games propagate) stand beyond the individual's capability to perceive that reality. In phenomenological theory perceptions of the world develop like snapshot views (Heidegger's mediation) and revelations (Peirce, 1998), thus making immobility an illusion, a fiction (Bergson, 1950; Adey, 2010, p. 5; Tzanelli, 2011, chapters 2 and 5). This observation propels us to investigate the relationship between (Olympic) categorical and (national) allegorical imperatives in depth – or, to be more precise, to unpack interconnections in contemporary ceremonial scripts, which are structured on cinematic principles.

1.3   Olympic articulation

Olympic ceremonies allow the co-existence of stasis with mobility so as to promote disparate 'articulations' of humanity. Human stasis and mobility in cinematic-like Olympic ceremonies mythologise (literally stage) leisure and work routines by presenting them as a form of timeless 'habitus', a set of embodied, behavioural and cognitive skills into which humans become socio-culturally inculcated and which they struggle to forsake (Bourdieu, 1977). Habitus and 'character' may be specific to cultures but work and leisure habitus can also function as universal abstractions. To be more specific, habitus might have emerged at a particular moment in the life course of the host city-nation; but for the needs of the Olympic show it is performed like a sacred fairy tale conducive to the categorical imperative, as it has to make sense on a global scale. All hosts have to have effective *diforic* (or *multiforic*) mechanisms in place to stage work and leisure routines in their national specificity. The consumption of Olympic artwork by global audiences in audio-visual and olfactory ways allows for the productions of new meanings in the global show of our mechanical era (Benjamin, 1989). No Olympic show would happen these days without extensive use of advanced technology and digital mechanics. Much like art, technology is broadly understood as 'a process

DOI: 10.1057/9781137336323

of social and cultural instantiations of ideational innovation' (Fischer, 2004; Fischer et al., 2008, p. 521). Technology and art form a mobility complex that is 'poetic' (it creates anew in embodied and machinist forms), multi-sensory and discursive.

My poetics connect to ideas of work, labour and art in specific ways. I draw upon Honneth's (1979, 1991) critique of the early 'culture industry' thesis, in which rationality is de facto instrumental. Artistic creativity has practical and poetic dimensions that allow for the production of a dialogics where objects and ideas become fixed by power centres (Wolff, 1984, pp. 126–8). In the following section I speak of 'travel art' in the Olympics extensively to advocate a model of articulation in defence of the new mobilities paradigm. Mobile articulations connect to spectacles of modernity such as expos and other mega-events in which samples of 'human specimen' were exhibited to global visitors for the first time (also Pred, 1991). Significantly, 'articulation' is borrowed from the lexicon of music to convey the formulation of transitions and continuities between multiple notes or sounds. Just as Said's (1994) post-colonial 'contrapuntalism', 'articulation' promises to transform the mediation of different viewpoints into a methodology of knowledge (Chowdry, 2007, p. 103) ingesting different ethnic idioms into the technological machine that institutes dominant forms of artistic idioms. Articulation's allusion to the act of bending one's joints (Latin articulation from *artus*, Greek *árthosis* = connection, joint, from *arthrōnō* = verbally articulate) also corroborates the embodied dimensions of nationhood via visions of human maturity and subjectivity (Tzanelli, 2011, chapter 5). Articulation is an audio-visual manifestation of literacy: the term's Indo-European roots (*arta*) speak of organisation akin to that of Greek *kósmos*, 'an iconic expression for "good order"' (Sandywell, 2011, p. 152). In the age of nations the paradox of literacy, in its print and audio-visual forms, was that it democratised knowledge while making it complicit to the emergence and preservation of political centres (McLuhan, 1962 and 1964; Anderson, 1991). Let us not forget that *ars* is the Western European rendition of Socratian *téchne* of *maieftikí* (literally midwifery), the ancient Greek self-searching method that bequeathed us Freudian psychoanalysis (Harrington, 2004, pp. 9–15).

The origins of touring in European colonialism (Grand Tour) stand as reminder that combinations of touring with art were not devoid of typological divisions of humanity (Hibbert, 1969; Towner, 1985; Gourgouris, 1996; Urry, 1996). The Olympic Games originate in Eurocentric myths of

DOI: 10.1057/9781137336323

the healthy body politic and the idea(l) of masculine whiteness as constitutive of global civility, just as tourism originates in Northern European
mobilities of the upper classes. The democratisation of both in the twentieth century did not remove this background. We may include in such
typologies the international migration of sporting talent and labour,
encouraged and facilitated by the social and economic undercurrents of
globalisation. These 'sporting nomads' move from host city-country to
host city-country and from one organising committee to another, accu-
mulating new knowledge but also leaving some of it behind for the locals
to use (see Maguire and Falcous, 2010). Of course the artists of Olympic
ceremonies are not athletes, but the homology is indisputable. It is precisely the cinematic projection of this homology that allows categorical
and allegorical imperatives to converge in Olympic art.

Let us begin with some observations on the status of Olympic artists
before proceeding to examine that of Olympic audiences. Bauman's
(1998) distinction between Southern 'vagabonds' and Northern 'tourists'
is rooted in the socio-linguistic traces of Europeanised antiquity and
provides a useful starting point. To make his observations more relevant
to Olympic art, I examine vagabonds as a rendition of the peripatetic
stranger who endeavours to satisfy his theoretical (*theoría*: technological
renditions of God's view) needs (Vardiabasis, 2002). In Europeanised
Plato's *Kratylos* this sort of vagabond roams the world looking for the
Truth – a futile exercise, given that 'truth' is in the eye of the beholder.
Viewed through Bauman's typology, Olympic artists operate as anomic
alítes, ego-enhancing theoreticians that conceptualise the world via
a camera-like mourning vision (see Harrington, 2004, p. 194 on postmodernism). Post-modern theory examines this phenomenon in connection with the ways the journeyman's and woman's mobility partakes,
voluntarily or not, in two diametrically opposing forms of power, the
nomadic artisan and the state architect (Deleuze and Guattari, 1988). The
book focuses on articulations of the first type, which may nevertheless be
mobilised by state power. It looks at the ways in which the 'mobile multi-
tude' (Hardt and Negri, 2000, p. 212) of elite creative-worker nomadism
articulates within systems of power the search for liberation and the
production of utopian visions. In its various experimental models, other
volunteers and non-elite folk join (Olympic volunteers, consumers and
audiences), thus pluralising the auteurs' articulations.

Today, the *theoría* of Olympic artists slowly moves away from the
exclusive Hellenic-European history of the Games through interactive

DOI: 10.1057/9781137336323

media play that supports a sharing mode with visitors to the Olympic city (Bernstein, 2000). Ranciére's (2011) analysis of spectatorship helps us understand how this play works: he claims that in any political movement passive audiences of spectators and the living principle of an active community must become one so that their experience is not merely mediated. But overcoming the gulf separating passivity from activity – or, in Ranciére's terms transform ourselves into 'emancipated spectators' (2011, p. 13) – is cut short by the reality that everything is mediated, and those who mediate are privileged citizens, armed with note books, cameras and stories. The 'knowledge gap' is confirmed every time narratives develop behind the lens as marketable items and mega-events become part of a stage that emulates (*miméte*) reality. Yet, staging Olympic allegories is today understood as a spectacle in its own right that audiences accept as participative simulation. Olympic post-tourists excel in playing social scenarios that are not real but invented for an ever-expanding basis of spectacle consumers (Liska and Ritzer, 1997). Kellner (2003, p. 66) reminds us that 'spectator sports have emerged as the correlative to a society that is replacing manual labour with automation and machines, and requires consumption and appropriation of spectacles to reproduce consumer society'. Unfolding the events for others and for oneself should lead to their de-mediation, bridging the gap between reality and fake spectacle.

These manufactured forms of agency unite through enactments of 'pilgrimages' that either refer back to the audio-visual matrix of filmmaking and other digital media or other embodied art such as acting, dancing and singing. London 2012 allowed for creative synergies of directors, actors and audiences and the co-production of new Olympic pilgrimages. Heretofore I use the neologism of 'synaesthesia' to capture this mind-body complex of performativity: deriving from a real disorder (synaesthesia as replacement of one sense with another), my 'performative synaesthetics' points to a productive re-ordering of narrative pathways through combinations of image, movement, touch, smell and sound (on performativity see Butler, 1993; on synaesthesia see Tzanelli, 2011, p. 19). These synaesthetic organisations of the ceremonies induce pilgrimages that combine the monetary capital of arts (e.g. the generation of tourism or other consumption styles) with the emotional and spiritual investment of artists and audiences in values that exceed this capital.

The link between the arts, tourism and the Olympic movement is pertinent because all three promote blends of what Nietzsche (1996)

DOI: 10.1057/9781137336323

saw in the Apollonian and Dionysian 'spirits', or intellect and emotion respectively. Where we usually acknowledge Nietzsche's dark European legacy of racism (e.g. the Nazi staging of Aryan Olympism) we may also discern the beginnings of neo-humanism in which leisure attains the role of a human right, a scholarly endeavour shared by Olympic and Paralympic athletes and audiences of all creeds and cultures, and which is simulated in the Olympic spectacle. In a revisionist Aristotelian streak Lanfant (2009, p. 105, p. 113) discussed the significance of *scholé* in tourist development as both study (first meaning of *scholé*, subsequently reserved for middle-class tourists) and free time (second meaning, associated with proletarian 'waste' of paid holiday). Much ink has been spent on definitions of tourism and travel and their relation to modernity. For the purposes of this book I distinguish between 'travel' as an activity and 'tourism' as an industrial phenomenon, but prioritise the co-existence of post-pedestrian, *mechanically enabled* mobilities with non-representational movements of thought and emotion that relate to variations of human 'work' (for the debate on industry and automobility see Urry, 1995, chapter 9). It seems then that even tourist theory has to resort to abstractions of work and leisure – abstractions that chronologically coincide with the establishment of Olympic ceremonies as a global spectacle in the post-war era (Guttman, 2006, p. 701; Roche, 2006, pp. 266–7). Such changes were further hybridised in the artistic orientation of the London 2012 directors, who figure as professionalised students and teachers of the cultures they render intelligible to global viewers in their popular and elite forms.

One may highlight that *scholé* as the ancient principle of self-perfection through intense engagement with arts such as drama or philosophy and athletics, culminates in synergies of body and mind, which underpin the contemporary Olympic phenomenon. Just like ancient drama, which was geared towards audience pedagogy through audio-visual and kinaesthetic enactments of *húbris* (human arrogance displayed to Gods), contemporary Olympiads are world theatres in which human aspiration to perfection instructs audiences about the values of fair play (Aristotle, 1946 and 1996). Notably, my Aristotelian philosophy is not grounded in the belief that a set of instantly identifiable 'ancient Greek' ideals are de facto European. Instead, I consider Aristotelianism as a journey through Hellenic, African, Middle and Far Eastern theories and theosophies that can never be 'recovered' as they were – especially in the British context of post-industrial modernity

DOI: 10.1057/9781137336323

(see also Nederveen Pieterse and Parekh (eds), 1995; Richardson and Jensen, 2004; Nederveen Pieterse, 2012). The leap from world politics to artistic poetics is pertinent for a critical positioning of Olympic ceremony artists. Their mobile identity as world professionals adheres to individual expressions of tourist-like artistic anomie on which global 'industrial communities' are based (Blauner, 1964, p. 24 in Hesmondhalgh and Baker, 2010, p. 29). Their audio-visual technologies actualise a God-like vision that guides traditional understandings of pilgrimage and its modern permutations as a form of action in support of wellbeing. Here the slow and the fast aspects of mobility converge with the help of novel technologies, also for the benefit of artistic audiences. I will expand on this in the next section.

1.4   Labour utopia and the category of 'human'

Coupling artistic with athletic excellence stands at the heart of my analysis because both British and Brazilian ceremonies were framed by its makers as post-industrial narratives. Here we have another link between allegorical and categorical imperatives through abstractions of artistic and athletic work. Rooted in the practical philosophies of the Scottish and English Enlightenment, the teleological narrative of mobility promoted the scientific *ergonomy* (*érgon*=work, *nómos*=law) of industrialised modernity first. The initial prioritisation of industry's ergonomic principles sidelined the *ergopoetic* aspects of 'primitive' cultures, as well as their contribution to notions of civility. *Ergopoesis* refers to the *ergetic* ability humans display to learn while doing (Funkenstein, 1986, p. 290; Trey, 1992; Ricoeur, 2005, p. 157, pp. 260–2). We encounter *ergopoetic* action in organised ceremonies that populate nationalised memory and also in the artwork of global creative industries that operate within disorganised capitalist economies. The split between *ergopoesis* and *ergonomy* distorts divisions between 'artistic' and 'social' volition originating in Weber's differentiations of spheres of human action (Mannheim, [1936] 1968, pp. 292–309; Mannheim, 2003; de la Fuente, 2007, p. 413; Witkin, 2005). So, for example, Arendt's critique of the individualisation of action, which is not grounded in social co-presence and an agreement with others supported by dialogue (Benhabib, 1992), could also be read here against a critique of modernity's consumerist logic that leads to reproductive exploitations of work (Bauman, 2005; Davis, 2008, p. 56). One may

DOI: 10.1057/9781137336323

recognise in *ergopoesis* the human ability to create unique art (DeNora, 2000 and 2003).

However, the original split between *érgon* and *poesis* also consolidated ideas of 'human' on an ontological split between mind and body, with emotion left in a theosophical limbo. Repairing such a schism has been the utopian project of the Olympic industry that repeats every four years its programmatic statements of fairness, solidarity and global equality through both *ergetic* (athletic competition) and *poetic* (opening, closing and medal award ceremonies) rites of passage and rituals (Barney, 2006). This restorative repetition is based on the ways Western Aristotelianism digested Plato's tripartite ontological schema of Images-Psyche-Ideas. This schema corresponded to human soul's (Psyche) arrangement into *noetic* (*nous* as reason), *epithymic* (*epithymía* as appetite, desire) and *thymotic* (*thymós* as spiritedness, temper) properties. This compartmentalisation recognises *thymotic* properties as auxiliary to reason only when the soul is not corrupted by bad upbringing (Plato, 1974, 441a). Psyche's pure nature is manifested in its desire to reach Ideas, whereas the desire to inhabit the world of illusions is viewed as a sign of corruption. Later Freudian psychoanalysis (Freud, 1948, 1967 and 2002) re-packaged this discourse into the study of civilisational progress: instead of waging wars, enlightened connoisseurs trained body and soul to 'peacefully compensate *thymotic* urge through the consumption of the arts as well as sports' (Wenning, 2009, p. 93). Twentieth-century modernity completed the industrial circle by defining labour and leisure on the basis of socio-cultural identity. Whereas at the systemic level post-war *scholé* was recognised (1948) as a fundamental human right (paid holidays) (Dann and Parrinello, 2009, p. 38), consumption differentiations on the basis of socio-cultural status continued to maintain divisions in societies.

My detailed philosophical excursus has to do with the role of Platonic and Aristotelian vocabularies of human nature in utopian projects as articulations of our place in the world and our hope of constant betterness (Bauman, 1976, p. 14). The Western fear of a dangerous *epithymic* revolution by human labour is closely linked to humanity's civilisational downfall. This validated the control of labour's embodied properties, especially via the state's divorce of *thymos* from *eros* (Marcuse, 1955). But this civilisational project stumbled upon the progressive commoditisation of middle and upper-class ethos so other differentiation mechanisms had to be put in place (see Bauman, 2007 on contemporary transformations). Ideally, humans ought to act as *ánthropoi* (*ánō*: up

DOI: 10.1057/9781137336323

and *thrōskō*: stare at), beings aspiring to reach the upper level of 'truth' rather than *vrotoí* (*vivrōskomai*: to perish), fallen beings consumed by earth and consuming pleasure (Tzanelli, 2008b, p. 149). The solution was provided when human desire and emotion were safely channelled, amongst other places, in collective spectacles that could offer education and consumption. The Olympic utopia sits on this philosophical back-ground, because it advocates a peaceful, global, social movement that can only better humanity. Though a practical but also aspirational form of action, in more recent decades Olympism was orientated towards human perfection in competition via technological manipulations of the body. Olympic artistic creativity also aspires to human perfection via digital narrations and performances for a global audience. This is how the principles of labour and art achieve an amicable co-existence in contemporary cultural industrial domains: labour and art become a form of laboured art, an artistic *ergopoesis* that can only be achieved through virtuous 'suffering' even in consumption rites (Bakhtin, 1984 and 1986; Campbell, 2005; Urry and Larsen, 2011 on the 'tourist gaze'). In ceremonies we do not deal with common workers but with spectacles akin to the working-class utopia of tourism-related migrations in which standardised symbols of leisure such as sun and sea function as cultural capital and means of upward social mobility (Bott, 2004).

The journey of these concepts might have had a European Christian starting point, but the spirit of the concepts has been functionally adapted in secular societies. Hence, Olympic sports such as the Marathon have transposed Christian discourses of suffering in the contemporary domains of Olympic sports as a spectacle consumed through images, sound and emotion. Likewise, the original sacrificial tale of Phidipeiddes (Philippides), the ancient messenger of good news about the Persian defeat to Athens, appealed to the romantic spirit of the Olympic journey that first discarded its pagan origins and then its religious aura. In the first instance the tale produced a model of athletics akin to the anchorite mobility of pilgrims (Adler, 1992) who invested in *catharctic* (purifying) rites akin to those promoted by Aristotelian tragedy. As Campbell notes (2008: 25–8), such rites eventually projected our (self-) pity and terror towards the great unknown, death, into symbolic dismemberment of the god of joy, Dionysus. The physical and emotional hardships of contem-porary athletes retain only a pseudo-religious aura that consolidates their celebrity status in new commercial media networks and contexts (Frow, 1998; Smart, 2005). The Olympic Marathon traditionally completes the

DOI: 10.1057/9781137336323

four-year Olympic circle of competition, as its medal award ceremony is the last and most noticeable of the Games. It is a fine example of open-air competition that defies the dictatorship of speed and the corrosive environment of city life, and regenerates belief in the value of simplicity and slowness (Parkins, 2004; Urry, 2007, p. 78). The original schism between virtuous *ánthropoi* and consuming *vrotói* is repaired through rationalised modes of wellbeing and exercise as well as the televised proof that these can be generously rewarded (see also Featherstone, 1991).

Note also how the Olympic spirit was based on the motto 'Citius, Altius, Fortius' (Faster, Higher, Stronger). This *hendiatris* (*èn dià triôn*: one through three) is part of the Olympic categorical imperative that projects a human being in aspirational motion. The founder of the modern Olympics, de Coubertin, explained that the motto outlines 'a programme of moral beauty', with sport as an 'intangible aesthetics' (IOC, Opening Ceremony, 2002, p. 3). But in new market milieus even the virtuous humans of the Olympiad have to navigate a competitive tourist globe, enter exhibitions and trade in cinematic simulacra. It is therefore time to examine how such categorical abstractions fit into the overall narrative of Olympic art today. My argument further develops the idea of work, art and tourist leisure by examining the ways they become integrated in ceremonial Olympism.

1.5 Olympic *tórnos*, slow and fast: the *tornadóros*

My exclusive investigation of the two imperatives in the Olympiad conforms to the argument that art participates in society by differentiating itself as a communicative system that is self-subjected to the logic of closure while simultaneously advocating utopian openness to other closed systems, such as that of national memory (Luhmann, 2000, p. 134). More correctly, I follow the post-modern corrective that challenges art as 'the specific integration of perception into communication in the medium of binary code of beautiful/not beautiful' (Harrington, 2004, p. 200) while acknowledging its function in multiple social spheres. In recent decades Olympic sport has slowly slipped out of exclusive Western institutional control – a shift that complies with the argument that it has always been a global public 'good' (Maguire, 1999, p. 86; Rumford, 2007).

From Luhmannian theory I adapt the idea that art is *autopoetic* or self-creating from symbolisations based on workable systemic

DOI: 10.1057/9781137336323

models with homologous function, or from the remnants of other non-functional systems. Hence, my adaptation has three dimensions: the first acknowledges that art systems remain an interpretative venture capable of creating anew from social modes of belonging (Chalip et al., 2000). The mobilisation of such social modes usually attains a symbolic function akin to Mannheim's artistic volition, but might also become conducive to organisational models on which artistic-as-industrial communities are based. The omnipresence of 'family' as an image and a mode of being and creating in the 2012 ceremonies corresponds to contemporary artistic and social volition. Therefore, the Habermassian critique of Luhmann that highlights communications between systems and life-worlds is necessary for my adaptation. Within this rationale I place the second dimension that acknowledges the technological forms of post-modern art systems such as those of the Internet and cinema. As forms these systems may be autonomous but their context is fluid as it is controlled by human labour. For the third dimension of my adaptation I place the content of the Olympic ceremonies within the context of tourism. Tourism is conventionally understood as movement 'away from [a person's] usual habitat, of the industry which responds to his [sic.] needs [while considering] the impacts that both he [sic.] and the industry have on the host socio-cultural, economic and physical environments' (Jafari, 1987; Theobald, 1998, p. 8). However, the ceremonies' artistic volition presents a blend of 'home' and 'away from home' ideas as tourism for global audiences. Though exciting as an economic or social model, tourism is replicated in Olympic art primarily at the symbolic level. It is worth highlighting that all allegorical imperatives integrate local cultural idioms into universally accepted versions of nationalism and post-nationalism (Robertson, 1992). Before the digital boom, Roche highlighted the production of 'mega-event libraries' by cities hosting the Olympics (1996, p. 325). The proliferation of Internet domains in which city-hosts advertise their staging of such events as well the externalisation of advertising to multiple global agents in media industries that have their own interests to promote outside those of the Olympic city's transforms the host into a 'node' of business rather than a stable Olympic centre in a disorganised global capitalist environment (Lash and Urry, 1987, chapter 1).

On this occasion the infrastructural is reflected in super-structural and symbolic domains. Passing locality through the imaginary of the host city and both through the global prism reflects ancient Greek philosophy's

DOI: 10.1057/9781137336323

delinking of the city-state from territory and its re-invention as a narrative node in a networked globality (the human *oikouméne*) (Inglis and Robertson, 2004). My recourse to the slow temporality or *la longue dureé* of European (ised) philosophical heritage works as a gateway to contemporary 'fast' mobilities of tourism, information technology and the now digitised cinematic spectacle. Etymologically, the word tour is derived from the Latin, *tornare* and the Greek *tórnos*, meaning 'a lathe or circle; the movement around a central point or axis' (Theobald, 1998, p. 6). Theobald notes that this meaning changed in modern English to represent 'one's turn'. The suffix '-ism' used in 'tourism' is defined as 'action or process; typical behaviour or quality' while the suffix '-ist' denotes 'one that performs a given action' (Ibid.). Even if we consider tourism as a commodity (Hiller, 1976 in Dann and Cohen, 1996, p. 305) its essence appears to replicate the essentials of the industrial process. My own analytical contribution is the suggestion that the Olympic tourist imagination is an artworld promoting the cosmopolitan art of *tornadóros* (the Greek worker of the *tórnos*) or turner. I hinge this concept on the Olympic categorical imperative and on Arendt's (1958) slow and plodding man, *Homo Faber*, which serves in my investigation as the cinematic archetype of today's 'speedy' Olympic cultures.

My thesis generates an essential link between 'slow' categorical and allegorical imperatives on the one hand, and 'fast' post-national artistic innovations on the other. Considering the Olympic artistic tourist as a *tornadóros* is not a literal exercise or plain metaphor. Drawing on Harré's (1986) philosophy of social science, Zeitlyn (2003) notes that metaphors help us comprehend, whereas 'models often are taken to be (partial or incomplete) representations, hence involve some sort of claim about reality [but] they guide action as well'. The art of *tornadóroi* points to forms of action implicated in articulations of modernity and post-modernity. Just like regular tourists, they become specimen of new communities and 'neotribal' social formations (Maffesoli, 1996) that live beyond traditional kinship networks. As mechanical engineers and traditional labour, *tornadóroi* physically performed 'their turn' in industrial mobility complexes. As post-modern *tornadóroi*, Olympic travellers traverse in their narratives the world equipped with their senses but also their prosthetic gadgets (cameras, ipads and mobile phones). Their imaginative travels are projected onto idealised humans in their artwork to actualise a utopia akin to that of tourism-related migration (see also Garnham, 2000 on the utopian possibility of art).

DOI: 10.1057/9781137336323

The word's masculine form conforms to old connections between manliness and civilisation (Bederman, 1995) – a trend that feminist theories of spectatorship could easily connect to the domination of global film industries by male leaders. However, the London 2012 spectacle provides evidence of more recent revisions in cinematic and mega-events leadership, as London's and Rio's creative leaders included both male and female artists.

In a not so dissimilar fashion Parinnello (2001) discusses the role of such artificial prosthetics in tourist mobilities. Here I purport that as performers of *tornévo* (the mechanic sharpening of our senses) artistic directors, filmmakers, stage artists and generally artists with embodied skills simulate these journeys on the screen and the Olympic stage. However, the sheer involvement of artistic creativity in the process breaks the repetitive cycle of movement we observe in tourist activity. This paradox of slowness (projection of national histories and traditions) in fastness (their temporal and spatial compression and innovative re-arrangement in less than four hours) is also complemented by their progressive cultural hybridisation (on 'slow mobilities' see Howard, 2012, pp. 15–17). Ceremonies are often staged by renowned cinematic directors, who have both deep cultural knowledge of the Olympic host and the skill to toy, fragment and re-assemble rooted narratives on stage and on stadium screens. However, their artwork necessitates substantial contribution by others in adjacent artistic domains.

Olympic artistic *tornadóroi* share privileged forms of post-national citizenship with the Olympic athletes: elite sport is a transnational phenomenon that expresses local specificity while simultaneously exhibiting the universal commonalities of socio-cultural organisation (Giulianotti and Robertson, 2004). Who works on art and how, as well as what stories see the light of the day in Olympic mega-events and who consumes them are questions we ask in all relevant contexts of globalised consumption. A deep analysis of the London 2012 context merits careful analysis in a future publication by other colleagues. Yet, my macro-social analysis also has to acknowledge that the athletic and the artistic *tórnoi* activate interpenetrations of localities, centralities and globalities, enabling utopian visions of human solidarity (also MacAloon, 1997). Hence my model of Olympic *tornadóroi* adapts (liberal, socialist and radical) feminist observations on inequalities of class and status but also the complexity of 'gender orders' to contemporary mobility trends. Such trends suggest the replacement of old gendered poetics (men's prevalence in public

DOI: 10.1057/9781137336323

domains) with new ones stressing image-making and personal glamour as strategies of self-presentation.

The London 2012 ceremonies were a labour-intensive spectacle, turning viewers into pedagogical subjects and tourists. The meaning of the ceremonies was also labour-intensive: as narratives embedded in the history of British and Brazilian industrialisation but also timely depictions of its urban life and popular culture, they promoted sanitised visions of 'home'. One may claim that such visions appeal to the workings of official memory in so far as they rest on 'solitary amnesias', selective re-arrangements of the countries' past, present and futures that are symmetrical to official history writing (Tzanelli, 2007a). The ceremonies belong to what Habermas (1989c) examined as systemic social forces, the 'steering media' and capital. As both critiques and reiterations of British and Brazilian modernity, the ceremonies also projected the identities of their creators and enactors (e.g. the 70,000 volunteers, actors and dancers). The London Organising Committee for the Olympic Games' (heretofore LOCOG) aim to produce an inclusive Games was encoded in the content of the ceremonies with some degree of success. The principles of inclusivity are an ongoing debate in the British context, with critics focusing on Olympic legacies (sport as a democratised pedagogical enterprise, the meaning of the Cultural Olympiad, the national future of sports), but also the enterprise's economic (budget distributions across the country), geographical (relevance of the Games for the national periphery) and other developmental (the futures of Olympic development in London) limitations. Again, these considerations merit separate analysis in another context. Here it is important to add an alternative perspective on the workings of Olympic art that would place ceremonial manipulations of national allegory on apar with 'solitary amnesias' promoted by the state but qualify them on the basis of practical decisions that art theory terms 'shedding' (Faulkner, 2006 in de la Fuente 2007, p. 421).

Although shedding is used in art theory to discuss decisions that precede not only actual performance but also performative improvisations 'on the night', as joint creative activity, it should also be seen as a process of making ceremonies work within a given time frame. Hence, the exclusion of less palatable chapters from British history might be understood both as a political and an artistic act in different domains of human action. It is questionable whether artistic directors want to 'develop' the way policymakers do, and the extent to which their

DOI: 10.1057/9781137336323

projects converge, if at all. Olympic art exists both within the national and the transnational domain with multiple functions. Combinations of embodied performance and technological projection allow for Olympic artwork to enter global markets, just as any movie. As artists the London 2012 directors enacted forms of imaginative travel through their work in collaboration with colleagues and volunteers that partook in the actual ceremonies. Making, valuing and consuming art are therefore considered as commonsensical social processes, the things 'people do together' (Becker et al., 2006, p. 3). Becker (1982) first claimed that art worlds are renditions of common-place knowledge about the arts following their differentiations from the sphere of the religion and the state, which sustained modes of imagining modernity. Such differentiations were progressively assisted by a combined appreciation of beauty in monetary and aesthetic terms (Tanner, 2003). The ambivalence of these articulations eventually spills into the practical domain of Olympic art-making. Music in particular – an important organisational component of the narratives of the London 2012 closing ceremony and the Rio handover ceremony – overdetermined the ways the Summer Olympiad's art work was valued and consumed by its audiences. Nevertheless, the London 2012 musical tropes also articulated understandings of the identities of London and Rio as Olympic hosts. It has been noted that musical mediation in art highlights the synergy between score-makers, musicians, recorders, classical instruments and their digital renditions (Hennion and Latour, 1993). Yet, music also mediates visions of sociality just as most performing and visual arts (see Hesmondhalgh 2007a on music and emotion). The rationale and meanings of these creative synergies are core aspects of this book's theoretical investigation: is the Olympic ceremonies core story, their 'archplot' (McKee, 1999) not supposed to be one of kinship tribulations through time and space (what we know as nation-building [Tzanelli, 2008a]) – an actualisation of the host's allegorical imperative?

Tourist and broader social theory account for the role of insider views of culture as touring and post-touring experiences whereas art theory draws attention to the abstraction of key social values in aesthetic forms and their mediation through different forms of sensory perception (haptic, optic and somatic [Witkin, 2005, p. 59]). This down-to-earth approach to ceremonial Olympics has been at the centre of discussions concerning differentiations between folk, popular and populist culture and has guided London's and Rio's art. The production of a simulated

DOI: 10.1057/9781137336323

collage of idyllic and leisurely Britain in the opening and closing ceremonies is constitutive of their creators' situated (labour) identity as liminal subjects, operating neither completely inside nor outside the cultural perspective enacted in them (Tzanelli, 2012a and 2012b). Symbolic 'distancing' from their homeland is an essential aspect of symbolic creativity of imaginative 'touring', transforming subjects from members of an 'imagined community' into strangers, migrants and tourists (Spode, 2009). Desforges (2000) argues for a tourist 'Self' that is relationally and reflexively produced through personal biography and Williams (1965) attributes the uniqueness of creative workers to their dedication in transmitting their expressive journeys as 'experience'. We are back to the debate upon work and leisure-travel.

1.6   Olympic spheres: *art*work, travel, activism

Britain is one of the countries that promote elite labour mobilities in art and sport (on sport see Houlihan and Green, 2008). Significantly, the directors of the opening (Danny Boyle) and closing ceremonies (Kim Gavin and Es Devlin) are part of London 2012's native but highly mobile creative labour. One may consider this typologisation as an example of governmentality, the exertion of what Foucault called 'biopower' on populations through normalisations of classificatory categories (Foucault, 1994; Foucault, 2003). Nevertheless, artistic directors should not be viewed first as national subjects but as members of the new transnational 'epistemic communities', groups or networks of experts with shared beliefs or ideas about specific issues that might occasionally influence or be drawn into national and regional policymaking (Haas, 1992). Such prominent Olympic artists may also partake in other similar events outside their home country. Recently, it was argued that from Sydney 2000 an 'Australian Olympic caravan' sprang: that is, a number of Australian Olympic experts and consultants whose expertise were mobilised in subsequent mega-events – Olympic, Paralympic, Asian, Commonwealth, Pan-American as well as World Cups and World Expos (Cashman and Harris, 2012). But, contrary to the linear argument of such Olympic legacies, artists form their caravans before the Games and proceed to capitalise on them within or without their birthplace. For example, Chinese director Yimou Zhang, who also acted as principal director of the Beijing 2008 ceremonies, was first involved in the Athens

DOI: 10.1057/9781137336323

2004 ceremonies (Tzanelli, 2008b, pp. 502–3). In the third chapter I examine another such example within the London 2012 network.

Zhang's case suggests that the cinematic contingent should not be passed in silence. As Laura Mulvey notes, recent technological advances have further changed the economic conditions of cinematic production 'which can now be artisanal as well as capitalist' (2006 [1992], p. 343). A shift towards decentralised modes of commodification and cultural invention in capitalist societies (Thrift, 2006; Currah, 2007) ensures that such professionals generate Olympic artwork on the borders of national and transnational imaginaries. Such artwork has to appeal to various recipients in global, networked environments and multiple public spheres (Slater, 2002). Although professionalised and transnational, the 'Olympic caravan' does not discard old kinship attitudes and practices altogether but transposes them instead onto a global platform on which they fuse with other mobilities of custom. Not only do artists introduce past collaborators into new enterprise, they may also move on to new projects in actual family clans and kinship groups (see analogy in Herzfeld's [2007] conceptions of 'global kinship').

Some other traditional attitudes also die hard in transnational milieus: from sharing ideas to 'illicit borrowings' from peer projects, the *tornadóros'* artwork resurrects the original tale of mobility theorised by Marcel Mauss in terms of 'gift' and 'giving' (1954). Originally, 'gifts' would change hands within clans or consolidate pacts between them, but anthropology has illuminated how even in the twentieth century various forms of reciprocity, including theft of goods from others, conditioned social hierarchies (Campbell, 1964, pp. 206–7, 201–12; Herzfeld, 1985, pp. 163–205; Herzfeld, 2005). Such claims guide the institution of creativity through intellectual property regulation (Wall and Yar, 2010, p. 257), but the old tale of craft – as 'crafty' attitude – is never out of date. The note is of Kantian categorical significance today as an extension of the entrepreneurial spirit only *vrotoí* display. I will return to this discussion in Chapters 3 and 4, where I discuss how the networks of the closing ceremony influenced its finished artwork.

Network theory is of great importance for the success of the Olympic spectacle. The transmission of regionally and nationally inspired Olympic artwork I mentioned in the previous section is directed both inwards (to British viewers) and outwards (to the world). This ensures that Olympic artwork is in fact *art*work partaking in utopian actualisations of a, both ethnically fixed and globally mobile, 'public sphere'

DOI: 10.1057/9781137336323

(Habermas, 1989b; Thompson, 1995; Fish, 2003). Hence, to practically examine the mediatised genesis of an 'Olympic public sphere', we must consider the ways in which new alliances between artistic labour and craftsmanship nourish contemporary social imaginaries. In the parallel world of sports activism, Harvey, Horne and Safai (2009) employed the concept of 'alterglobalization' to explore the potentialities offered by sport to develop an anti-neoliberal, anti-neoconservative, anti-imperial or anti-capitalist alternative to globalisation. Not all these movements are radical or progressive, nor do they always promote the inclusion of individual polities in global communities: alterglobalisation can easily lapse into anti-globalisation (see for example Tzanelli, 2011 on *ressentiment*). One may question the relevance of such movements to the project of commercialised Olympic art, which can be either conservative or radical, depending on the socio-cultural context.

I approach the complexity of this issue from a slightly different angle, by stressing how the London 2012 opening and closing ceremonies were based on post-modernist fusions of art and craft, reason and emotion. Borrowing from the tropes of human nature to produce its own unique archplot (McKee, 1999, pp. 45–8), Olympic artwork is committed to conservatism that has little to do with political party lines a priori. There is no doubt that artistic sentiment stems from various political contexts, as does academic writing, but the expression of utopian universality often transcends the context prior to its interpretation (again, this merits separate consideration). Artwork is not a-political but cosmopolitical: first, we may note that Olympic Games might be used in various political contingencies by any party in power at the time of their delivery. Second, their artwork's content exceeds such concerns as it is open to multiple interpretations. Thirdly, we must distinguish between national and transnational nuances in such interpretative frames. Finally, we ought to examine closely Olympic artwork's 'human types' in context. For this reason, looking past narrow political intrigues, I use Castoriadis' (1987) distinction between the institutional and the radical (social) imaginary to examine contributions of Olympic artwork to the production of a utopian public sphere. Drawing on Benedict Anderson's (1991) account of the imagined community of the nation, Taylor points that social imaginaries are neither theories nor ideologies, but implicit 'background understandings' that make possible communal practices and a widely shared sense of their legitimacy (Taylor, 2004; Steger, 2008). New audio-visual markets operate as diagnostic domains for the causes and effects

DOI: 10.1057/9781137336323

of human disenchantment, promoting a hermeneutics of recovering and restoring human pasts in search for new functions. More controversially, individual studies highlight precarious collaborations and shifts between the two imaginaries in national domains. Even in tourism 'national domain' can be created through reflexive awareness, to produce a utopian spectacle consensually with global visitors (see Meltzer, 2001 in Franklin and Crang, 2001, p. 10, p. 13). Olympic venues are tangible aspects of such utopias too, because they bring together human populations otherwise divided by geography or politics.

National centres brand and appropriate art and architecture nevertheless. As a global 'travelling culture' changing hosts every five years, the Olympics both actualise and contest the meaning of the tourist *tórnos* (Christaller, 1955, pp. 5–6; Adey, 2010; Tzanelli, 2008a, p. 66). This is so because their function is both centripetal (looking to the birth of the Games in the imaginary centre of European civilisation, Athens) and centrifugal (looking outwards to the cultural varieties of humanity, in new host cities and new projected narratives of cultures). Every Olympic host aims to create a unique urban brand that is culturally specific and locally meaningful while simultaneously encapsulating universally intelligible ideas of the national terrain in which the Games take place. Because the brand has to be thoroughly professionalised, it establishes a symbolic distance from peripheral permutations of identity on which the national centre may continue to draw for political mobilisation in other contexts (Bourdieu and Nice, 1980; Lury, 2004). It has been argued that brands represent a lifestyle both cherished and under threat by modern forces, as much as they invite interpretative work by consumers (Holt et al. 2004). Stranded between 'heritage' as a form of intergenerational transmission and 'legacy' as a contract signed between the IOC and the prospective host, they have to negotiate the normative rules of *tórnos*. Once the Olympic Games are over, legacy turns into heritage for the urban host that has to learn how to capitalise on it (also MacAloon, 2003 and 2008 on Olympic legacies). This can only impact on what is presented in Olympiads as authentic and the strategies artists may even invent to evade stringent Olympic protocols. Clifford (1988) reminds us that cultural authenticity is constructed in a range of media and sites of representation, including popular writing and artistic production. However, whereas collecting and displaying various artefacts in galleries and museums eventually became part of a nationalised 'art-culture' system, the folk origins of these ethic routes usually figure in

DOI: 10.1057/9781137336323

public self-presentations as 'pop culture', and often sites and signs of cultural 'pollution' (Douglas, 1992, pp. 26–9; Douglas, 1993; Douglas and Wildaski, 1982; O'Brien, 2008, chapter 6).

In post-modern contexts ceremonial Olympism usually overcomes such dichotomies through acceptable harmonisations of 'art culture' and 'popular culture' systems, generating utopian hybrids that can then circulate as memory signs across time and space (Lash and Urry, 1994, chapters 6 and 9). Usually these signs become overdetermined by Western, European hegemonies that might allow them to enter heritage registers as 'pure' forms by signposting their hybridity as progressive. Such Olympic utopias are paradigmatic of a shift in production and consumption regimes that emphasises audio-visual 'anthropophagy' – the global circulation of conceptions of the 'human' as advertised by the distant cosmopolitanisms of film, television, print press, and the Internet (Tzanelli, 2012b). All media played an important role in the enactment of the London 2012 ceremonies, becoming auxiliary components of the system of Olympic mobility. Supplementing the classical paradigm of *homo oeconomicus* – describing the entrepreneurs of late modernity that turn themselves into their very own source of capital – with that of a *homo communicans* – the self-monitoring individuals that control their own image while paying tribute to other points of view – is constitutive of contemporary discourses of wellbeing but also of collective harmony (Foucault, 1997; Illouz, 2008).

The Olympic system on which host cities rest their brand produces novel knowledge economies from revisions of the old European economy of thought (Argyrou, 2013, forthcoming, chapter 3) in which communitarian ethics took precedence over individual will. This economy has presided over the Olympic event for centuries, consolidating oscillations between the functionalisation and re-symbolisations of the Games as a unique cultural gift to humanity (for perspectives on 'gift' and 'giving' see Sahlins, 1972 and 1976, p. 210; Berking, 1999, p. 127). The pluralisation of the host (Athens is one of the potential hosts) allows for the introduction of novel discourses of reciprocity to the original narrative of the pure Hellenic civilisational gift (the athletic spirit of beauty-as-harmony) (Tzanelli, 2004). Each donor to the world unburdens their obligation to reciprocate this gift by promoting their own civilisational contribution to the world. But as the circuit of reciprocity is open-ended and unbalanced (not everybody gives the same thing and nobody can reciprocate the original 'debt' to Athens), the European economy of

DOI: 10.1057/9781137336323

thought repeats its pendulum-like narrative every four years. Locked into an exchange of temporary complementarity rather than reciprocity (Gouldner, 1960 and 1973), individual hosts change their status by staging their own Olympic ceremonies. This staging allows for a shift from the trope of virtuous *ánthropos* to that of fallible *vrotós* that Eurocentric Christian traditions once condemned for his/her alleged 'devilish' Oriental properties (Campbell, 1964). One may also note that the move from perfect and virtuous to fallible and 'consumable' humans is part of society's attempt to 'tame' human mortality first through collective rites of remembrance and later through technologically mediated tropes of consumption and fandom (also Bauman, 1994 in Hviid Jacobsen, 2012, pp. 84–5). For this reason the Olympic spectacle and the organised Olympic protocol cannot escape the trauma of human mortality altogether but collectivise and refine it aesthetically instead in literary, musical and athletic forms (see also Woodward, 2012 on a different approach to athletic time). At the performative level, the imaginative travels Olympic ceremonies create conform to the principles of what is known in tourist studies as 'thanatotourism'. Thanatotourism or 'dark tourism' in and through public spectacles such as that of the Olympic ceremonies appeals to the practice of organised human visits to imaginary and actual locations 'wholly or partially motivated by the desire for actual or symbolic encounters with death' (Lennon and Foley, 2000; Halgreen, 2004, p. 149; Sahlins, 1996). Thanatotourist rituals are constitutive of the creation of new public spheres by cultural industries, their agents and agonists. At a structural level, such performances also allow for the regeneration of communities as the only way for humans to counter the solitude of individual and collective deaths. This is how generic narratives of human and his/her gifts are replaced by nationally specific ones, and how human giving enters a narrative of exchange within a global family akin to that of the crafty artistic 'neotribes'. My schema provides a template for the new mobilities paradigm and the theory of travel, embedding forms of agency in stringent structures and systems. Just like the urban host's function as an Olympic communicative complex, the new communicating human becomes a mobile subject willing to employ technologies of the body and the self for the production of a plausible public image in mega-events that stays behind for future generations.

The utopian togetherness of such thanatotourist rituals is merged with the ephemeralities of trade. Thus, the vision of reciprocity as memory

DOI: 10.1057/9781137336323

is transposed into the new virtual spheres of the Internet and cinema from which we can purchase its audio-visual and material (souvenirs) traces. In a similar vein, London's virtual narratives of the 2012 Olympiad supported the host's agential action, by borrowing from the spectacular cultures of the Orient to craft a European urban phantasmagoria (Patke, 2000, pp. 4–5). They based these narratives on subaltern identities that once supported the know-how national cultures, but fused those with other bohemian styles and 'folkish' customs. London's hybrid phantasmagoria was supported by its thriving arts scene, especially theatre and cinema that further valorise its global profile (here, virtual, embodied and visual mobilities go hand in hand). As an urban spectacle of late modernity (Debord, 1995), London's emphasis on the visual adheres to a tourist-like gaze that works from above and afar (Szerszynski and Urry, 2006), entrapping human action (creative work) in museum-like simulacra (Edensor, 2004). Following suit, the ceremonies' digitised utopia (heretofore 'digitopia') developed as both a centripetal and centrifugal (mobile) narrative in London's strategic articulations of identity. Emphasis on global contributions by London-as-Britain to the promotion of global technologies in the ceremonies is such a strategic move. For example, identifying the birth of the World Wide Web solely in Berners Lee's work promoted one interpretation over others. Another version would stress the role of European Organization for Nuclear Research (CERN), Switzerland, as the institutional environment in which Berners Lee worked as a contractor. Notably, Berners Lee himself provides a more nuanced account of the invention as a synergy that ascribes to the post-national tale of industrial networks (Berners Lee, undated). The opening ceremony's emphasis on his own role could be considered as part of Danny Boyle's 'shedding' decision or as a strategic alignment with the host's self-narration (indeed, it is the official LOCOG guide to the opening event that attempts this move rather than the director). The cosmopolitan profile of London that, whatever Britain's actual policies on ethnic plurality, is irrevocably multi-ethnic and multi-cultural is strategically filtered through utopian fusions between Western and Eastern habits.

London's mobilisation of the once disreputable Oriental practices of economic transaction with an emphasis on fair and sustainable profit-making (on which see Kopytoff, 1986) exemplifies this happy merger between old economies of thought and action and the principles of fair communication (Urry, 2008). Ideas of recycling and also virtual

DOI: 10.1057/9781137336323

communication emphasise technological manipulations of nature and provide a specific vision of sustainability suitable for the 'developed' world (see Urry, 2011, pp. 151–4). London 2012's online shop for purchasing all manner of items celebrities left in the Olympic Village subscribes to the self-help mode of funding from 'refuse' (O'Brien, 2008). The craft of bargaining and bidding on items used by athletic celebrities is an embedded feature of the Olympic digitopia. Traditional crafts habitually become part of nationalised and commoditised folklore that is 'associated with the emergence of national consciousness and glorified as the repository of ancient skills' (Herzfeld, 2004, p. 5). But as a global city London is amongst the leaders of the digital revolution and in a position to influence modulations of craft that now place emphasis on the electronic mastery of goods (Internet). Like artists, digital *technítes* (artisans) belong to the human capital that partakes in this transformation of a long-standing *Historikerstreit* exemplified by the Habermassian battle to rescue repressed pasts into a *Materiellestreit*, a dispute over the London Olympiad's material mobilities (Habermas, 1989c). Haggling and bidding on Olympic items touched by the aura of athletic celebrity re-articulates the phantasmagoria of the ceremonies, allowing them to function as tourist souvenirs (Kohn and Love, 2001; Fraser and Brown, 2002; Stone, Joseph and Jones, 2003; Malfas et al., 2004, p. 213). More importantly, digital marketing of London 2012 tokens partakes in the articulation of public discourses that 'frame' visits to places 'repeatedly mark[ing] the boundaries of significance and value at tourist sites' (Neumann, 1988, p. 24). In short, the promotion of Olympic tokens on the web replaces the old ghosts of heritage with digitopias of virtual cosmopolitanism (Rheingold, 2000; Dyson, 1998; Hand and Sandywell, 2002; Tzanelli, 2011; Yar, 2012).

1.7   Chapter outline

In the next three chapters I analyse the technological synergies of artistic creators, actors and ideas in the Opening and Closing Ceremonies of London 2012 and the Rio 2016 handover ceremony. Each chapter works as a unity that fits into London 2012's totality of refined art and pop craft. Despite any localised artistic closures, the narrative of the book is open-ended and no 'conclusion' can be reached. By the end of Chapter 4 it will become very evident that any conclusion merely generates new questions

DOI: 10.1057/9781137336323

and challenges only future artists can answer. As a result, the book does not include a concluding chapter, as it is not intended as a closed narrative.

Chapter 2 explores the opening ceremony as an audio-visual narrative of British culture. It is argued that its synaesthetic modes both activated and contested organised modes of nostalgia for British pasts rooted in rurality but also its destruction with the advent of the Industrial Revolution. The centrality of pop pastiche conformed to ideas of home, land and belonging but turned those into a global landscape. The event was framed by technology as Britain's contribution to the world – a discourse that conforms to motifs we encounter in the European economy of thought. Boyle's articulation and the host city's articulation were built on the transcendence of folk ideas of *téchne* and the adoption of digital craft that can manipulate 'national character' on the big screen. The co-existence of (emotional, ideological and technological) mobilities with stasis replicated the working of the Olympic *tórnos* as leisure, tourism and labour.

Chapter 3 suggests that the directors of the closing ceremony produced a musical narrative for the host city that corresponded to the performances and stories of the opening event. The centrality of leisure, tourism and work in representations of London conformed to urban tropes of lifestyle mobilities with a global appeal. The ceremony's structural organisation and display of artists with personal connections in the Olympic industry butalso the propensity to embrace what appeared to be banal conceptions of tourism and work crafted abstract ideas of kinship. Just as the opening ceremony's juxtapositions of the time of everyday life (*chrónos*) to Olympic sacred time (*kairós*), the closing ceremony's artwork synthesised a post-modern spectacle based on the co-existence of slow and fast mobilities. These combinations defined London and Britain as a concrete place, an imagined national land but also transnational 'space' in the Olympic temporal bubble.

Chapter 4 provides an in-depth textual and contextual analysis of the handover ceremony to Rio. The staged performances are examined as marketable revisions of Brazil's colonial history that lead to the artistic display of ideal types and characters for global audiences. It is suggested that the backgrounds of political revolt and oppression in the country assist in the ceremony's artistic 'autopoesis', the repetitions of culturally situated *leitmotifs* and patterns as mere (consumable) 'signs'. As the Brazilian anthropophagous project is placed in the hands of privileged natives (artistic directors), it becomes a valorisation vehicle. For this

DOI: 10.1057/9781137336323

reason Rio's artistic archplot was based upon exotic interiorities and marginalities (black 'racial types') that correspond to the 2016 host's vulnerable or uncouth modes of social being (samba dancers, capoeira and Candomblé performers, 'bad men' and glamorous white women). The ceremony's articulation enmeshed all these types and styles into Rio's self-presentation as a tourist topos that was born out of past mobilities of humans, customs and embodied narratives of labour. In post-industrial environments all these inform lifestyle choices.

1.8   Epistemological and methodological foundations

It should go without saying that any analysis of art is an articulation in its own right (see Williams, 1974). One could argue for a 'double hermeneutics' (Giddens, 1987) that grinds down the details of the artistic spectacle and performance and then assembles them anew in this book. However, the Giddensian schema might simplify what is a plural, polyvocal enterprise undertaken by multiple actors (artistic directors, journalists and broadcasters, ceremonial performers and finally scholars) in multiple media domains (the TV, the Internet, personal computers and books). McLuhan's (1962) hot (intense concentration, strict control) and cold media (participatory) blends in such dialogical networks is paramount for our understanding and methodological use of the enterprise. The communication of relevant staged events is not mediated for the sake of media networking per se (Giddens, 2002; Urry, 2008). However we see this, the medium is both the message and its mediation, enabling various actors to reconstruct a technopoetic grammar and social researchers to analyse it (Van Dijk, 2006). In our digital era there is no way we can neatly distinguish between orality and digitality (Ong, 1982) and our hermeneutics end up looking more like another layer of travel, another mind-walking rite and additional emotional labour. In this respect, Archer's (1995) open model of human interpretation and its examination of anthropological epistemologies (Archer, 1996, pp. 4–22) provide another rigorous frame that complements Giddensian hermeneutics. Music in particular would necessitate an adaptation of such hermeneutics so as to include non-representational analysis that does not display the ideological propensities of denotative media such as literary and visual arts (Born and Hesmondhalgh, 2000, p. 2). However, the present book does not deal with the psychic worlds of music audiences

DOI: 10.1057/9781137336323

as such (an impossible task to be sure, as music speaks to individual inclinations and emotions), but with the *mobilisation* of popular genres in ceremonies to represent specific cultural genres. As all cultures lack a 'fixed core' (e.g. Žižek, 1991, pp. 234–44; Žižek, 1999, p. 18), and both global markets and emergent regional differences always revise hegemonic fixities, it may be more correct to consider music in Olympic ceremonies as a hermeneutic vehicle constitutive of the artistic *tórnos*. My starting point is always a multiple hermeneutics of being human that attains specificity in different contexts and by particular human mediators, including artistic directors and performers. This allows for a flexible combination of the fluidity of cultural form with the fixity of performative intentions (Born and Hesmondhalgh, 2000, p. 5). Therefore, how music is felt is by necessity placed on a continuum with how and why it is used and communicated in the 2012 Olympic ceremonies, and also how such mediations draw upon its spatio-temporal depth. This depth is split between custom/experience (intimate uses), history (official uses) and global mobilities (marketing to others). To do so, music is treated methodologically as 'hyperconnotative' (Ibid., p. 32) – a blend of text (lyrics), sound and performance, a vehicle of intersectional conflicts or collaborations (e.g. race, gender, ethnicity, class) but also a medium for emotional expression.

Considering such theoretical contributions, I proceed to propagate a dialogical schema of interpretation (Bakhtin, 1984, pp. 252–3) via combined actors in the drama and disparate mediations. Serre's and Latour's (1995, p. 118) conception of angelic communication that immerses us in celestial informational fields and transmission systems already points to the imaginary origins of the hermeneutic venture (Hermes, the winged God of messaging) (Tzanelli, 2011, p. 30). This privilege of travelling the Olympic world 'from afar' (Szerszynsky and Urry, 2006) via multiple new media routes and roots actualises a public sphere that is more decentred than a few decades ago (Poster, 1995, 1997; Cavanagh, 2007). But although this enables the production of interpretive frameworks for social action independently from state-controlled ideology it would be naïve to claim that it eliminates the power of hegemonic narratives (Melucci, 1995). I am aware that the minds of those attending such events are beyond grasp but the model of communication is within my reach and can be used here. I recognise that any discourse analysis does not constitute in itself developmental policymaking (Nederveen Pieterse, 2011, p. 239). My consideration of an increasingly fragmented 'European

DOI: 10.1057/9781137336323

economy of thought' in Olympic artwork suggests that I do not prioritise the political economy of the Olympics. I suggest instead that Castell's network society model (1996) in which 'nodes' direct information flows has to be re-thought in the context of cosmological flows in Olympic artwork. Here the overlap of various 'scapes' (Appadurai, 1990) or flows is streamlined primarily through hegemonic ideas (of Europe as an Edenic topos) that can both challenge and reinstate other hegemonies (e.g. of capitalism or nationalism).

Although these observations are not in themselves conducive to my methodological technology, they guided my focus on audio-visual interpretation: acknowledging the presence of multi-directional flows of ideas via multiple networks suggests the existence of artistic plurality even within hegemonies, de-centring even my own flimsy auteurism. Thus, I acknowledge that my own aesthetic judgements of Olympic artwork might be inspired by a projection of labour modes (originating in the social milieus of underprivileged *technítes*) onto the lifestyles of privileged artistic leaders (working in contemporary cultural industries). The model of the *tornadóros* is a hermeneutics of recovery reminiscent of socialist histories. However, any such militant sympathies take a back seat when artistic creativity and innovation open up to multiple resources, audiences and readers: what I 'canonise' in my book and what others retrieve from my thesis is part of a much wider intertextual network which we cannot surrender to monocultural political agendas (Sarlo, 1989, p. 22 in Popovitch, 2011, p. 46). Because the *tornadóros* is first and foremost an interrogator of originality as an incremental feature of post-modern creativity, (s)he resembles academic scholars when it comes to interpretation.

Following a renouncement of my post-modern type's aesthetic pessimism I try to capitalise on mass-mediatisations of artwork and on inter- and cross-textuality in my research. Websites such as those on Wikipedia may have to be treated with caution, but as productions of information nodes they remain useful. Hence, I used the Wikipedia pages on the London 2012 opening and closing ceremonies as guides to national and international press coverage on the events, but also for their hyperlinks to other Wikipedia information nodes on artists and Olympic personalities. My media sources also included video posts of ceremony fragments on You Tube and the BBC news website; whereas various image stills from Flickr and other open access sites supported my visual interpretation. Based on my theoretical take of hegemony and

DOI: 10.1057/9781137336323

pluralism I treated image, sound and text as a unity to follow the artistic models of interpretation that I unpack in the next three chapters. Such 'texts' are tied to socio-cultural contexts as their disconnection from them would produce an impoverished analysis. Just as artistic directors and performers, I look to a 'dialogics of recovery' of pasts but proceed to examine possibilities of blending them into present needs and modes of thought (Ricoeur, 1984, I, p. 61; Bakhtin, 1986, p. 106; Habermas, 1989a, pp. 226–7; Bell and Gardiner, 1998, pp. 6–7). The futures of methodological thought on Olympic ceremonies tap on to such a transition from mono-sensory to multi-sensory analysis, from viewing to listening and doing, or what Sandywell (2011, pp. 75–6) discusses as a model alternative to the Eurocentric construction of the world as a 'mega-visual' order (Fuller, 1988; Jay, 1993). The book may be loaded with visual testimony in the form of images and lack auditory or performative sources due to practical restrictions (copyright regulations and the immediacy of embodied performance), but it considers the artwork of the London 2012 mega-event as a multi-sensory resource. Thus, thinking between 'high' articulations and 'low' manipulations, I craft a narrative of ceremonial flows ready for new interpretations.

DOI: 10.1057/9781137336323

2

The Opening Ceremony: Structural Nostalgia and Pop Pastiche

Abstract: *This chapter explores how the Opening Ceremony both activated and contested organised forms of nostalgia for British pasts rooted in rurality as well as the destruction of rurality with the advent of the Industrial Revolution. The centrality of pop pastiche (humorous artistic narratives of cinematic and national characters or personalities) conformed to globalised ideas of home, land and belonging. The event was framed by digital technology as one of Britain's contributions to the world. Specifically, it transcended folk ideas of technology in favour of new digital crafts (Internet, cinema) that can manipulate 'national character' on the big screen. The co-existence of (emotional, ideological and technological) mobilities with stasis (ideas and ideals fixed in time) replicated the working of the Olympic* tórnos *as leisure, tourism and labour.*

Tzanelli, Rodanthi. *Olympic Ceremonialism and The Performance of National Character: From London 2012 to Rio 2016.* Basingstoke: Palgrave Macmillan, 2013.
DOI: 10.1057/9781137336323.

2.1   The technological human: biographies and objectives

Across the world, the opening ceremony commanded respect and excitement often combined with puzzlement and disdain, with varied commentary in major newspapers and blogs such as *Washington Post*, *New York Times*, *NBC*, the Japanese *NHK*, Italian *Rai*, German *Frankfurter Allgemeine Zeitung* and many more in India, Brazil and the African continent (Topping, 27 July 2012). The London 2012 Organising Committee of the Olympic and Paralympic Games produced a special guide (2012), which praised the show for its successful reception by the city's administration, the Queen and the IOC. Titled after a Shakespearean quote from *The Tempest* ('Isles of Wonder'), the ceremony chartered aspects of British culture, including the Industrial Revolution, and various contributions of drama, literature, film and technology to global culture. Shakespeare employed the *hendiatris* in *Henry V* and *Julius Caesar* to circumnavigate the main characters' ethical mobility, from immaturity to self-knowledge. The plot of character development is constitutive of de Coubertin's Olympic *hendiatris* too, which produces an embodied cosmopolitan aesthetics. Later in the chapter we will examine how this leap from the individual to the collective and from land to landscape – cinema's *techno*logy or artistic rationale – attains cosmological proportions when the Olympic Rings literally circumnavigate the earth at the end of the ceremony. Without copying chapters from the Beijing 2008 spectacle, Britain's technological centrality in print-capitalist channels formed an even transition from Chinese to Western representational plains via a universalised discourse on reciprocity. However, the latter chapters of the show became progressively more about global cultural flows and hybrid projections of belonging.

The director of the Opening Ceremony, Danny Boyle, is a fine example of those blends between embodied craft and visual art examined in the previous chapter. Born in 1956 in Radcliffe (Lancashire) into an Irish Catholic family, he rejected priesthood for a career in drama. Years later he noted a 'real connection' between film directorship and religiosity because 'there's something very theatrical about it. It's basically the same job – pouncing around, telling people what to think' (Leach, 14 January 2009). Boyle's determination to move into the world of performance was realised with his early employment as director in the Royal Court Theatre and the Royal Shakespeare Company and as director for the

DOI: 10.1057/9781137336323

BBC Northern Ireland. Boyle's epistemic network progressively moved from kinship-orientated to post-traditional professional connections that today extend to Hollywood. Becoming known in the mid-1990s as director of films such as *Shallow Grave* (1995) and *Trainspotting* (1996), in the first decade of the twenty-first century he proceeded to direct commercial films such as *The Beach* (2000), and the multi-award *Slumdog Millionaire* (2008) and *127 Hours* (2010). These later landmarks betray an interest in the experiential dimensions of travel mobilities: the liminality and insularity of backpack travel enclaves of the Orient, adventurous slow travel as a root to self-discovery and Westernised representations of poverty in the developing world as charitable attraction to repulsion (Stallybrass and White, 1986; Tzanelli, 2006). Boyle's artwork allows us to analyse tourist spaces as 'more than representational [...] simultaneously both visually engaged with but also embodied through the concept of performativity' (Adey, 2010, p. 146; Dickmann and Hannam, 2012, p. 1316).

The tendency to experiment with Western mediations of the Orient in non-representational terms (through feelings and experiences) guides the preponderance of hybridised memory in Boyle's Olympic artwork. Both re-asserting and contesting Western hegemonies, his technological creativity re-thinks relationships between structure and agency through the propagation of embodied and digital forms of *flânerie* to actual human pasts and presents (Nash, 2000; Giddens, 2002; Thrift, 2007; Tzanelli, 2011, 2012a and 2012b). The omnipresence of the discourse of pastiche in Boyle's artwork agrees with his dialogics of recovery. Based on the principles of parody, pastiche has been discussed both as an empty 'blank parody' without political content (Jameson, 1991, pp. 16–17) and as a genre that subverts fixed attitudes to history and habitus (Hutcheon, 1989, p. 101), sharpening the artistic subject's reflexivity (Hutcheon, 1988, p. 122). Derived from older stylistic hybrids (Italian *pasticcio*: medley but today also a meat-pasta dish), pastiche is a sort of medley that creates identities for mass consumption – just like family tourism advertising. Boyle's pastiche of cinematic characters that have become associated with an undefined 'British' *longue durée* was based both on intimate and professional knowledge of such 'characters' that can open up to ideological critiques of hybridity in post-modern artwork (Hoesterey, 2001). It may even be argued that Boyle's cinematic pastiche conforms to shifts we notice in various Olympic brands from tropes of heritage to those of legacy. These recurring themes underline the opening ceremony's

DOI: 10.1057/9781137336323

'archplot', the central scenario that sustains unity of action within the story (McKee, 1999, pp. 3–4, pp. 41–2). This archplot reiterates Olympic themes of betterment, the human-technological body as well as the principles of reciprocity that once thrived under the techno-scientific banner of European modernity (Yar, 2012, p. 182). Boyle's tendency to employ a hermeneutics of recovery in the first half of the ceremony was complemented with his futuristic dialogics of various art forms in the latter part. Jokingly put, the priest had shed his garments for a pop outfit and performance.

'Isles of Wonder' was framed as a story on the British revolutions 'that changed the whole world', with the Industrial Revolution 'rebooting human existence' (Opening Ceremony, 2012, p. 11). The emphasis on the creativity, exuberance and generosity of the British people centred upon 'the digital gift' of British scientist Tim Berners Lee, the creator and distributor of the World Wide Web. The discourse of giving which generally underlines the Olympic Games was also framed by previous hosts in terms of cultural capital (Bourdieu, 1997): the overriding objective in a gift economy is to give away resources to secure and retain status (Currah, 2007, p. 475) – in London's case, to demonstrate abundance in digital resources and the power to distribute them as gifts. Belonging to the colonial peripheries of the previous centuries, Australia (Sydney 2000), Greece (Athens 2004) and China (Beijing 2008) narrated their contributions to the world in similar cosmological-cultural terms. As opposed to their prioritisation of 'culture' over 'civilizational' excellence (Chatterjee, 1986, p. 20; Chatterjee, 1993, pp. 5–6; Tzanelli, 2004, 2008b and 2010a), Boyle resorted to the old colonial rhetoric of technological innovation to frame British unconditional giving by temporarily erasing the realities of (online) transaction from what followed Berners-Lee's first 'open access' act. Reciprocity is the privilege of Baumanesque 'travellers' who can afford to circulate an 'excess' of ideas and goods in global networks of distribution (Bataille, 1988). At the same time, the mobile and ephemeral nature of digital Internet cultures bypasses the colonial legacies of failed reciprocity, crafting in their place a new ideal type of British citizen as a world traveller but also a new ideal type of Olympic viewer as a *virtual flâneur* (see also Tzanelli, 2012a; Germann Molz, 2004, p. 171). The Olympic spectacle as a whole looked to the futures of such outlived pasts by introducing other twenty first-century participatory technology. The mega-event's introduction of 'audience pixels', 70,799 small panels mounted between seats, corroborates this symbolisation

DOI: 10.1057/9781137336323

of global togetherness on a giant screen extending around the audience seating area. Centrally controlled, this human-machine computer was auxiliary to all Olympic and Paralympic ceremonies' audio-visual complex, as its coloured lighting coordinated with music and stage performance. This allowed Boyle and his team to treat attending human subjects and assisting mechanic technologies as a unity (Thrift, 1996; Urry, 2000).

The co-existence of national moorings with virtual mobilities (Hannam et al., 2006) was extended to other scientific and *techno*logical advancements, including a glamorised representation of the National Health Service (NHS – a 'common good') and the development of a mechanical world of popular culture. Flagging volunteering as a British initiative (Opening Ceremony, 2012, p. 12) also contributed to the discourse of reciprocity and tied the moral principle of care to nursing and to tourist service through the ceremony's performances. I return to this issue in the specific section of the ceremony. For the moment, it is worth noting that the volunteers (publicly honoured for their contribution at the end of the closing ceremony) are the perfect example of the Olympic transformation of spectators to actors and the creation of alternative 'cultural movement networks' (Oppenheim, 2003 in MacAloon, 2006, p. 25). The very priority of LOCOG on long-lasting infrastructural 'legacy', with the creation of an Olympic Park in the former 'under-developed' Lower Lea Valley (East London) reproduces the ideals of care, sustainability ('One Planet Living') and reciprocity. Considered as a whole, the opening ceremony's 'dream of universal communication' (Opening Ceremony, 2012, p. 11) is a perfect example of articulation through fusions of old and new cultures of mobility (Sheller and Urry, 2006).

The memory of reciprocity is a global good constantly changing human hands: Greece continues to head the Athletes' Parade in the Olympic Stadium and the Greek flag is still part of the formal handover from one host nation to the next in the closing session. As much as London 2012's opening ceremony was haunted by the memory of the opening ceremony of the 1948 Games at Wembley Stadium in a country ravaged by war, its broadcast qualities of mourning also became accommodated into discourses of neo-pilgrimage (novel commoditised pilgrimage to sites deemed to be 'sacred') as tourism (Tzanelli, 2013: chapter 3). Edensor argues that 'tourism is a process which involves an ongoing (re)construction of praxis and space in shared contexts' (2001, p. 60; also Graburn, 2001, p. 151), and so constantly involves

DOI: 10.1057/9781137336323

'performances' and places that depend upon the performances that take place within them (Bærenholdt et al., 2004; Thrift, 2007). The global social imaginary was modelled by Boyle upon the European imaginary of suffering associated with the cameraman's God-like *theoría* but also with the formulas of adventure and backpack tourism (Cohen, 2011). The leap from individual to collective pilgrimage was enabled by a repository of 'signs' upon which the opening ceremony developed as an audio-visual 'performance' (Lash and Urry, 1994, chapter 9). The European economy of thought is today a global economy of human suffering binding the spectators and audiences through distant, broadcast messages (Kyriakidou, 2008). The sacralisation of such global memory landscapes in digital domains emphasises the diversity of 'roots' and 'routes' in imaginative travel (Clifford, 1997).

Boyle's appointment to this task makes even more sense if we consider that one of LOCOG's priorities has been to bring back home and revive the Paralympic Movement (Peoples' Daily, 30 August 2012). The televised campaign of London Paralympics as a 'Superhuman' effort by the successful broadcasting bidder, Channel 4, revised discourses of equality and public recognition through extensive daily interviews and reports on Paralympian athletes and the movement as a whole. Notably, these 30-minute programmes drew heavily upon the ongoing recruitment for future Paralympics from the pool of rehabilitated war amputees (implicitly compared to the superhero comics genre). Boyle's artwork fits into this formula in lateral ways: his award-winning directorship figured the imaginaries of war and personal disaster (the crypto-colonial narrative of Western travel in *The Beach* was filmed in Thailand that is haunted by the Vietnam War; *127 Hours* narrates a trekker's self-amputation experience). This attention to the politics of (im)mobility, or rather to how movement is represented and experienced (Cresswell, 2010), also connects to his Olympic artwork that manipulates a different form of (im)mobility connected to Britain's peripheral cultures. It has become commonplace practice for activism to amass its organisational tools and human networks in digital domains because they defy time-space problems (Cere, 2002). This malleability of cyberspace – broadly defined here as the space of cosmological governance – allowed various major Olympic players to suggest to a pool of global fans that they can figure as actors rather than spectators of the Olympic movement by technopoetic means (videos, photos and press interviews posted online on blogs) (Yar, 2000, pp. 1–3; Chouliaraki, 2008).

DOI: 10.1057/9781137336323

2.2   Scene-by-scene

The *Countdown* to the event was projected like a film that takes audiences through some of London's iconic tourist markers, using Thames as a network of sights (MacCannell, 1989). An array of literary and kinaesthetic signs (from *Wind in the Willows'* Ratty and Mole to the Oxford and Cambridge boat race, the House of Parliament and Downing Street's door to the Rotherhithe Tunner) are mediated through the countdown numbers that lead to the stadium. The same arrangement of signs will re-appear at the end of the closing ceremony, to complete the Olympic 'circle'. Amongst such tourist signs we also view the most iconic artefact of the city's leisure domains, the 'London Eye': literally a circle associated with the cultures of vaudeville theatre, the circus and also the carnival of American Expos, it will also re-appear in the closing event. Not only does the *carnivalesque* of the artistic ceremonies assert Olympic athleticism's sacred unity and its tourist-like liminality in this way, it is also staged like the plot of a typical Hollywood movie: its end corresponds to its beginning, re-instituting everyday time through the conventions of a happy ending (Turner, 1969; Bakhtin, 1968, pp. 255–7; MacAloon, 1978; Clark and Holquist, 1984, p. 302). Meanwhile, in the stadium children popping balloons on each count eventually release the five Olympic Rings attached to four balloons that will carry them to the stratosphere. The connection of celestial to the Olympic movement conflates mechanical and tourist mobility (Urry, 2007, pp. 27–8). Childhood innocence is repeatedly mobilised in the ceremony as a symbolism of Olympic biographies: humans accomplish maturity through ceremony.

It is telling that the countdown culminates in the sounding of the Olympic Bell, the largest of its kind that will remain in the Olympic Park for the next 200 years. The bell was specially made for the occasion in the Whitechapel Bell Foundry, a historic workshop that made Big Ben (1858) and Liberty Bell (1752). Via sound and image this introduction already links traditional to digital craftsmanship through Londonese understandings of 'cockney' (literally born within the sound of bells) (Opening Ceremony, 2012, p. 19). The material incorporation of 'cockney' into the ceremony might correspond to a symbolic incorporation of East End marginality into the city's self-narration while 'forgetting' the realities of poverty that historically characterised these urban neighbourhoods. In this respect the bell symbolises the taboo that white – that is privileged – epistemologies represent as an aestheticised tourist-like

DOI: 10.1057/9781137336323

FIGURE 2.1   *The Olympic bell*
Source: Elizabeth Harkin/Flickr

souvenir. However, linguistic semantics also connect to auditory semantics, as it is traditional for Big Ben to announce the coming of the New Year and for church bells to stand for both freedom and danger. This cultural overlaying culminates in another reference to Boyle's autobiographical influence by Catholic cosmology, which arranges religious rites around olfactory and auditory habits. In his artwork such rites have been transformed into cosmetic signs and adages without losing their symbolic value altogether. Cohen's (1992) suggestion that self-knowledge and social knowledge of people are often incongruent, and Fabian's (1983, p. 93) observation that the presence of our past in us often takes shape as 'a project', converge behind Desforges' (2000) recognition of travel as an autobiographical tool. Boyle's artwork is exemplary of a here-conscious and there-semi-conscious 'mind-walking' (Ingold, 2010) which he can successfully share with a global community thanks to its iconic form. 'Walking' through childhood experience in adulthood commands, according to Carruthers (1998, pp. 109–10, p. 251), a 'mnemothetical perambulation' akin to craftsmanship. It is precisely this autobiographical

DOI: 10.1057/9781137336323

mind-walking that facilitates the use of theatre techniques as a source of intercultural knowledge, transforming every visit to Olympic artistic sites by the native or historically informed tourist into a sort of multi-sensory 'participative mimesis', a performance of experiences with inte-grative qualities (Fabian, 1999, p. 28). The significance of the Olympic Bell is also overlaid by LOCOG's official pronouncement of the London 2012 Olympiad as the 'austerity games' and a journey 'against a backdrop of dramatic social and economic change' (Opening Ceremony, 2012, p. 5). The sound of danger and freedom neatly correspond to the risk of austerity and the pleasure of the Olympic Games.

The '*Green and Pleasant Land*' section of the ceremony also looks to utopian blends of fact and fiction that historically informed both proc-esses of nation-building and tourism mobilities. The Britain it projects is the one created in *Winnie-the-Pooh* and the *Wind in the Willows* – literary perambulations of an Arcadian British universe in which natural won-ders are simply the order of the day. These fabulist animal personae that entertained several British generations are domesticated versions of wil-derness. It is not coincidental that the section's centrepiece performance in the stadium involved a meadow in a green circle filled with cottage houses, animals and farmers tilling the soil while sport was played on the grass and families enjoyed their picnic break. The segment complies with the ways the tourism industry markets a particular version of Englishness 'in which the country is caught in a time-warp and people comport themselves as a folk' (Samuel, 1989: iv in Palmer, 1999, p. 315). The mediation of the national body's primordialism through images of peasant agriculture is linked to animal domestication: the 'talking' animal characters of fairy tales have always been integrated into house-hold activities, becoming thus part of an enlarged family economy that encourages the development of anthropomorphic metaphors of 'being' a friend or a brother (Levi-Strauss, 1964; Heidegger, 1967; Barthes, 1993; Tzanelli, 2011, chapter 4). European countries look to landscapes as cultural heritage steeped in legend, mythology and history but the transposition of them into the big screen also triggers new processes of meaning-making (Prentice and Guerin, 1998; Edensor, 2004; Edensor, 2005; Thompson-Carr, 2012). Far from projecting a narrow understand-ing of national labour, the scene speaks the language of original leisure – hence, the beginnings of Western civility in Britain's agricultural settings. Rather than reproducing the habitual 'denial of coevalness' (Fabian, 1983, p. 39), the Olympic ceremony turns the historical lens inwards, to

DOI: 10.1057/9781137336323

England, to achieve the temporal co-existence of different worldviews within the British nation.

The tourist spectacle is a sort of mind-walk: Urry speaks of 'places that die' (2004, p. 208) to explain the shift from *land* (tangible forms of *Heimat*) to *landscape* (its transformation into an ideal based on novel technologies of the eye). The shift marks a replacement of concerns with the ways representations are produced, conserved or modified (Mitchell, 1994). To consolidate the combination of embodied and cinematic tourist experience for viewers, four films from around the UK follow the 70-day journey of the Olympic Torch, enhancing the feel of the Olympic neo-pilgrimage. Choirs from each of the four 'sites-sights' of the British imagined community actualise this tourist synaesthetics: 'Londonderry Air' from Giant's Causeway, Northern Ireland, 'Flower of Scotland' from Edinburgh Castle, Scotland, 'Bread of Heaven' from Rhossili Beach, Wales and 'Jerusalem' from London in the Olympic Stadium. These symbolic songs were performed by singing clubs and choirs from the four sites (Belfast Philarmonic and Phil Kids Choir, The Big Project Choir, Only Kids Allowed, Only Vale Kids Allowed, the West National Orchestra, and the Dockhead Choir). As forms of untamed wilderness, Wales, Ireland and Scotland partook in productions of a civilised national identity, and as major tourist destinations today they have become central to marketisations of the British margins ((Mackenzie, 1997, p. 70; Edensor, 2005; Bolan and O'Connor, 2008). Their iconic natural beauty cannot but shape the British utopia of the ceremonial section.

This audio-visual neo-pilgrimage's crescendo is definitely the face-to-face performance of William Blake's (*Milton*, 1804) 'Jerusalem'. Inextricably linked to the divorce of humans from nature with the onset of the Industrial Revolution (Lienhard, 1999), the poem was adopted by socialist and conservative interest groups over the centuries as a sort of supra-political manifesto on labour (see Hodges, 24 April 2012). Facilitating yet another circular cinematic tourist journey the phrase 'Chariots of Fire' and the corresponding film became part of the best cinematic encapsulation of the Olympic spirit. The roots of the anthem in English Protestantism suggest that Boyle uses colonial discourses of a fictionally uniform British identity in his artwork (Tzanelli, 2009, pp. 52–3; Poulter, 2009). At the same time, the emphasis on working-classness produces an audio-visual discourse on cultural intimacy that frames the British allegorical imperative. 'Cultural intimacy' (Herzfeld, 2005, p. 3), the self-acknowledged aspects of one's vulnerability to external spectators

DOI: 10.1057/9781137336323

(tourists, media), demands vigilant supervision by the community that claims monopoly in its selective commoditisation. Bestowing British labour with dignity and presenting it as part of the national soil is a strategy that enables national valorisation and visual commoditisation. The strategy is *diforic* because it rests upon the gendered discourses of honour and shame that operate as principal civilisational binarisms in other cultures (Peristiany, 1965; Herzfeld, 1980; Davis, 1987; Tzanelli, 2011, chapter 2): national labour is dignified and ennobled, not something to hide from the public eye but pure and authentic. The choral yet young focus of the musical background consolidates the primordial epos of the journey, and the segment's thanatotourism connects the British community to the post-religious cult of nationalism (Tzanelli, 2008a, p. 146). Thus, the labour of national memory work (Gabriel, 2004), at once intimate like a feminine entity and childish like a being in need of guidance, joins a global mobility matrix in felicitous pedagogical ways.

The performance of the Shakespearean line '*be not afeard – the isle is full of wonders*' by Kenneth Brannagh who impersonates the character of Isambard Kingdom Brunel, Britain's most revered engineer, also contributes to associations of British land with tourist landscape. Just as Shakespeare is deemed to be part of England's heritage, its Arcadian staging in the stadium and on the big screen are connotations of national land-as-landscape. This artistic dialogism produces the nation's 'integral ideational position' (Bakhtin, 1984, p. 252) – a statement that sustains its elective mission to civilise others (Tzanelli, 2008a, chapter 6). As the Shakespearean speech is underscored by Edward Elgar's 'Nimrod', land-as-landscape also connects to the memory of war. The Opening Ceremony (2012, p. 20) points out that the background music has become associated with wreath-laying at the Cenotaph on Remembrance Sunday for the contribution of servicemen and women in the World Wars. Here the ethics of mobility become entangled in the paradox of nostalgia, the angst of the journey 'back home' that haunts the literary scene of Western high modernism (Gibbons, 2007, chapter 1). Remembering from a cinematic distance is an experiential journey to sites of memory that are both personal and collective (Nora, 1989; Huyssen, 1995; Urry, 2004, p. 209; Gibbons, 2007, pp. 2–3). The trope refers to old Grand Tourist itineraries, their professionalisation (travellers as colonial administrators) and its implication in chains of media production (Seaton, 1999, p. 132; Tzanelli 2008a, chapter 4). It is therefore not a surprise that the section concludes with the ground being ripped open to the sounds of

DOI: 10.1057/9781137336323

FIGURE 2.2   *Depictions of the Industrial Revolution*
Source: Shimelle Lain/Flickr)

drumming: the following Industrial Revolution is born in British land, from its native labour.

But the next section, '*Pandemonium*', is not just about the rise of industry but also the story of the first organised social movements in the country. Just as Bloch's modernist pathos, the narrative in this section suggests that utopias are based on collective labouring creativity that propels humans to the future (Thompson, 2012, p. 38). Hutchinson observes that nation-building may involve an 'inner' activist movement to crystallise notions of the past, but it also necessitates the 'external' creation of a cult of sacrifice 'by a revolutionary elite' (Hutchinson, 2004, p. 109). Originating in Milton's capital city of Hell in *Paradise Lost*, the section nicely reflects through the tale of British industry both the human fall from Paradise and the Promethean theft of knowledge from Olympic gods – two archetypal stories overlaying the emergence of an 'Olympic Industry'. The initial pandemonium on the stage that includes ripping off the grass, the emergence of giant industrial chimneys, and the migration of rural populations to the first urban centres are suddenly succeeded by silence. Silence allows for an existential journey to begin and a mobility pathway that slowly pushes viewers outside the

DOI: 10.1057/9781137336323

inner activist circle. On the stadium's giant screen a symbolic reference to cultural manipulations of British 'nature' takes us to a poppy field that a group of soldiers stare at in silence. In Britain the poppy has become part of a post–Second World War adaptation of Armistice Day – today known as Remembrance Sunday (11 November 1918). The main ceremony of this commemoration takes place at the cenotaph in London where it is attended by thousands and broadcast by the BBC. The ritual and its global broadcasting sketch a 'British nation' united in grief for this massive human loss. Clashing with Britain's ethnic polyvocality, in which being 'multiculturalist' and 'multicultural' do not always agree (Parekh, 2000), this national event is often disrupted by protests of anti-military groups, unemployed ex-soldiers or Muslim organisations. One may see in Boyle's (preceding) industrial 'Pandemonium' a metonymical intervention in Britain's socio-cultural landscape. Hinting that the British national 'core' is unattainable, Boyle and his associates make some interpretative space for the Olympic spectator without relinquishing the fact that the country's national broadcaster, BBC (incidentally, also the director's professional affiliation), is involved in the Olympic spectacle. One may claim that the particular and the universal co-exist in the ceremony's segment: the audience is prompted to join the stadium's soldiers in remembering the dead of all wars. This is symbolised in Boyle's artwork through the Accrington battalion of the legendary Somme. However, the visual narrative is overdetermined by a natural sign of exceptional significance in Protestant Irishness – a striking incorporation into a ceremony directed by an artist that grew up in a strict Catholic environment. The Unionist cult of the poppy in remembrance rites of the First World War that has joined nationalising narratives of Irishness (Poulter, 2009 and 2013, forthcoming) has also spilt into a post-colonial imaginary of consumption in sports and other forms of leisure. Its association with early clashes over Irish sovereignty and social movements becomes reinstated and diluted in Olympic narratives, where the poppy becomes a 'sign', a travelling culture and a tourist commodity of situated significance (Barthes, 1993; Lévi-Strauss, 1964, pp. 26–7). The inward and the outer national voices built a community of pilgrims and the specific places of mourning acquire global significance. Cenotaphs are popular tourist sites as much as they are sites of memory, after all (Nora, 1989): by replacing all the scenic Welsh and Scottish landscapes that the BBC includes in Remembrance Sunday's live broadcasting (another borrowing in the Olympic ceremony only

DOI: 10.1057/9781137336323

native viewers recognise), London's cenotaph can become another naturalised 'sign', just like the poppy.

The adjacent ceremonial parade of the trade unionists fighting for worker's rights, the Suffragettes who fought for women's voting, traditional Pearly Kings and Queens and the Beatles who represent the 1960s social movements, generate a British audio-visual and kinaesthetic vortex. This ceremonial kinaesthesia enmeshes people into ideas of land, only to transform both into a touring landscape for Olympic visitors. Boyle makes an open connection between feminist, industrial activist causes and the rise of an Olympic movement, which is literally crafted by industrial labour in the Olympic Stadium. It has been suggested that artists and activists alike are socio-culturally disposed towards a particular type of social action that questions social norms and values and grants them with a form of pedagogical agency constitutive of bourgeois radicalism. This 'radical habitus' (Crossley, 2003, p. 45) is symptomatic of the 'submerged networks' and 'abeyance structures' that keep radicalism in constant flow through various mobility channels. Where historical evolution seeks to abolish history 'by relegating to the past, that is to the unconscious, the lateral possibles that it eliminated' (Bourdieu, 1998, p. 56), artistic activism resurrects the past in creative ways to remind us of our obligation to bring doxic imperatives to the sphere of discourse (Tzanelli, 2007a, p. 254; Habermas, 1996). Unsurprisingly then the segment of the ceremony ends with the uplifting of five man-crafted giant rings to the field of play, thus reiterating both the Olympic categorical imperative and the allegory of British activist nature.

The epic music is a form of neo-pilgrimage to a multi-cultural space that draws upon recorded ethnic technologies of immense market value in the global leisure trade (Graburn, 1983). The music was composed and directed by Rick Smith of the innovative electronic duo Underworld that collaborated previously with Boyle in *Trainspotting*, *Sunshine* (2007) and *Frankenstein* at the National Theatre – an example of artistic networking (Opening Ceremony, 2012, p. 22). Devoid of lyrics, harmonised sound backgrounds selective kinaesthetic narratives of the country. External audiences cannot fathom the geographical coordinates of Boyle's Industrial Revolution, but an informed viewer can detect a discreet shift to Northern parts of the country. The cradle of the Revolution and Boyle's birthplace, Lancashire (and Yorkshire, where some of Boyle's artistic networks extend or from which they originate), become covert autobiographical nodes in the segment. The sequence is nevertheless

DOI: 10.1057/9781137336323

FIGURE 2.3   *The 'rising' Olympic Rings crafted by industrial labour*
Source: Shimelle Lain/Flickr

DOI: 10.1057/9781137336323

enveloped in contemporary electronic rhythms by Underground to counter rootedness. Traditional mechanics (the foggy chimneys that emerge from the ground, as if they are part of British nature) and post-modern engineering (musical instruments) form a unity. The sequence's archplot of human development encloses a form of 'structural nostalgia' (Herzfeld, 2005, p. 150) for a world lost to human (post)modernity – a world nevertheless accessible in its cinematic form. Here Baudrillard's (1983) simulation theory takes precedence over social realities, staging alternative cosmological visions that might resemble actual civilisational forms without ever identifying with them.

The actualisation of such technopoetic synergies in a renowned global city should not go unnoticed: urban phantasmagorias addressed to terrestrial and virtual tourists, web surfers and cinematic audiences enclose to horror of the unknown, the 'stranger' that traverses such urban domains and destabilises fixities of tradition (Bauman, 1991, p. 56; Kristeva, 1991, p. 8). The cosmetic nodes of the city as a museum for ethic specimen and a safe stronghold produce a social meta-genre (Tudor, 1976; Langford, 2005, p. 167) in which ideas of 'threats' and 'risks' are never quite managed by technology. Beck's (1999) 'risk society' is enacted in this segment through conflations of the unknown in new social movements, the 'dirt' of industrial labour (O'Brien, 2008) but also an ever-present intimacy of culture that all national imaginations hold dear. It is precisely such domains that cultivate intercultural communication, as they are both prone to external stereotyping and to marketisation. At such conjunctions 'community' and nation-state might overlap in terms of social action to enable both interpretive achievement by independent actors and political mobilisation by the national core (Habermas, 1989a, pp. 118–19; Delanty and O'Mahony, 2002, pp. 50–3). Due to its cosmopolitan character artistic labour provides the tools of such mobilisation, also outside the national domain, making intimate cultural narratives part of global mobility chains. This is tourism writ large, as a vehicle of the artistic imagination that can recreate national labour – the British nation's first internal migrant groups – on stage. The very depiction of industrial labour crafting the Olympic Rings amidst the fumes of the Revolution reproduces the basic thanatotourist principles that Dann (1998, p. 37) and MacCannell (1989, pp. 54–9) recognised in the transformation of working-class unwholesomeness and stiffness into a mobile consumption object. This segment is the ceremony's narrative node because it appeals to the rise

DOI: 10.1057/9781137336323

and development of a new popular culture ethos initially dismissed as vulgar and kitsch (Theobald, 1992, p. 76; Binkley, 2000) but eventually accepted as a sui generis articulation. It also appeals to Victorian understandings of working-classness as the pure domain of nationhood (Tzanelli 2011, chapter 6). These performances certainly link to Britain's thriving 'heritage industry' as a tourist attraction (Dann, 1996; Urry and Larsen, 2011, p. 137), but may also carry another allegorical meaning: the stadium nestles at the heart of what used to be an industrial site, a wasteland the Olympic project aspired to regenerate as a leisure/athletic hub. The ceremony re-articulates the memory of labour and its ethos: it (f)uses working-class and athletic subjects to project the ideal *Homo Faber* on the screen through an unwritten pact forged under the capitalist conditions of our late- or post-modernity (see also Buroway, 1979; Debord, 1995). The artistic allegory speaks the language of recognition through a global spectacle that adheres to the moral grammars of tourist labour. The ethics of work frame industrial humanity's self-image as a community of carers while also defining its relation to leisure economies. Leisure economies enable cultural mobilities that ought to be beneficial for cultural givers and native workers – if not, they might construe mobility as bad practice in the first place (Derrida, 1994; Derrida and Dufourmantelle, 2000). We come full circle now, as the Olympics' gift economy is predicated on mutual respect between natives and hosts (Tzanelli, 2011, pp. 133–5).

'*Happy and Glorious*' is the section that accompanies Queen Elizabeth II and the Duke of Edinburgh's entrance to the stadium, alongside IOC President, Jacques Rogge. The Union Flag is also carried into the stadium by the Royal Navy, Army and Royal Force. Significantly, the national anthem is sung by the Kaos Signing Choir for Deaf and Hearing Children, an award-winning integrated project for children aged between 4 and 18 (The Opening Ceremony, 2012, p. 24). Appealing to banal images of primordial nationhood (by analogy to Billig, 1995), the anthem's embodied complex allegorises inclusivity in the British polity. Part of the Olympic protocol and pageantry, the rite commands respect by British citizens and global audiences. However, the cinematic sequence that precedes it clashes with its seriousness, casting Boyle's artwork as quintessentially *carnivalesque*: on a giant screen in the stadium we watch a film shot in Buckingham Palace in which the Queen is visited by Daniel Craig as James Bond. Together they mount a helicopter that aerially traverses the city in the familiar tunes of the cinematic genre. As

DOI: 10.1057/9781137336323

the helicopter steadies over the Olympic Stadium and James Bond opens its door we watch the 'Queen' to parachute out, followed by Bond. The 007 theme from the days of *Dr No* (1962) is played in the stadium and the Union Flag opens up in front of the Royal Box to reveal the Queen. The film thus exchanges the screen's distant aerial shots with the proximity of the Queen's entrance purposedly: generally the detective (literal and cinematic) genre appeals to tourist mobility (Reijders, 2011), but the James Bond films in particular have embraced the tourist logic through their ubiquitous inclusion of exotic destinations throughout the world (Tzanelli, 2010b, p. 55). However we see it, the 'comic' film suggests that in London the Olympic site and the stadium are exotic domains which even the Head of the State has to inspect 'from afar' and 'from below' so as to domesticate them. And yet, the mediatised tale issues a reminder of the impossibility of this venture in the context of sacred, televised time.

One may put a break here and ask how from a linear narrative of modern British history we moved to this discourse. The functional role of this segment seems to disrupt tradition and to transfer audiences into a stage in which no story can be told in conventional ways. Just as the Olympic Park's simulated labour in 'Pandemonium' this comic disruption becomes 'a mythological sheath for the idea of development – but one that unfolds not so much in a straight line as spasmodically, a line with "knots" in it, one that therefore constitutes a distinctive type of *temporal sequence*' (Bakhtin, 1981, p. 113). If the hypothesis is correct, we should not question the focus of the next section ('*Second to the right, and straight on till morning*'), which honours aspects of labour through two British 'technological achievements': the body of children's literature and the National Health System (NHS). The shift from the crafts of home to public technologies integrates these achievements into Olympic leisure time through acting, singing and dancing. Founded in the post–Second World War era (1948) on Aneurin Bevan's principle that 'no society can legitimately call itself civilised if a sick person is denied medical aid because of lack of means', the NHS is overlaid in the ceremony by the labour of family work. The segment's scenes project a normative feminist theory of care and of non-contractual values such as trust and responsibility (Deacon, 2007; Kittay, 2001; White, 2003; Williams, 2002; Williams, 2004) but eventually replace those with the professionalisation of nursery in institutionalised medicine. Embedding this ethics of family care into the British medical system creates a link between bodily politics and the politics of identity.

DOI: 10.1057/9781137336323

Although the body is a suitable site for the expression of cultural sentiments (Douglas, 1993; Foucault, 1979), *like* the ethnic 'essence' of a nation-family it remains a natural property (Tzanelli, 2008a, chapter 7). As a result, Olympic artwork attempts to restore what has been lost in a governmental biopolitics that remains determined to extract the 'bio' from its politics (Herzfeld, 1992; Foucault, 1997; Tzanelli, 2011, chapter 5). Placing the NHS volunteer staff into discourses of Olympic volunteering and childcare also suggests other connections to philanthropic travel commonly known as 'voluntourism'. The ethic of professional mobility that emerges from Boyle's audio-visual spectacle uses the ambivalent language of this type of tourism as an adventurous lifestyle in combination with the activist empathy defining the NHS foundation (Hall and Williams, 2002; Hall et.al., 2004; Simpson, 2005; Benson, 2011). We need only consider that, just as the NHS, Olympic volunteering was proudly advertised by LOCOG as a British contribution to the Games dating back to the 1940s (Opening Ceremony, 2012, p. 12) – a statement that reiterates the Olympic gift economy.

On stage dancers spell out with their bodies the initials NHS and GOSH for Great Ormond Street Hospital, a London hospital for children to which J.M. Barrie bequeathed the royalties from his masterpiece *Peter Pan*. Hundreds of beds with children overseen by volunteer nurses from the NHS flood the stage, and a girl is pictured on the screen reading literature under the bed sheets as Mike Oldfield plays 'Tubular Bells'. A 'horror' atmosphere is created with a series of nightmarish villains from literature (Voldermort, Cruella de Vil, Captain Hook and the Queen of Hearts) that appear in the stadium as giant puppets. Britain's most loved nanny, Mary Poppins, dances in multiple human copies on stage to banish children's nightmares from the story. A cinematic persona as much as a literary character, Poppins exemplifies the global shift to technological mediations of experience. Julie Andrews, who impersonated the character in the most popular version of the musical (*Mary Poppins*, 1964) was also tied to discourses of philanthropy as early as in 1970 (Beck, 28 August 1970). Andrew's long-standing connection with London's theatre and arts scene also situates her within the city's biography and network (Academy of Achievement, undated). But we must also account for Andrews' insertion into another network of cinematic tourist references through her salubrious performance in *The Sound of Music* (1965). As Graml (2004) explains, this musical re-mapped Austrian identity abroad through the hybrid simulacra of Julie Andrews as Maria Trapp, the film's

DOI: 10.1057/9781137336323

children, and the iconic images of Austrian landscapes that boosted several large- and small-scale enterprises in the country. Austria's failed application for the 2010 Winter Olympics, titled the *Sound of Winter Sports*, drew on such global articulations of Austrianness when within the country national identity would mainly be defined by Mozart. But whereas such Austrian tendencies to cultural closure might have fostered anti-globalisation sentiments (Tzanelli, 2011, chapter 3), Maria Trapp travelled the world, changed into Mary Poppins and inserted herself into discourses of the 'nation' in another country that successfully hosted the Olympic event in 2012.

The presence of novelist and known philanthropist J.K. Rowling in the segment bridges the gap between literature and its cinematic adaptations – a popular trend in today's film production. Rowling's presence might be construed as another critical intervention in the ceremony, given the author's social profile as a single parent that had to live on welfare prior to her fame with the *Harry Potter* novels (Bio.truestory, 'J.K. Rowling', 2012). Her ambivalent social profile as a middle class entrepreneur with a difficult background is all the more effective in this artistic context. Rowling's reading from *Peter Pan* is intended as a celebration of the human communicative abilities (Opening Ceremony, 2012, p. 26), but the very act of bedtime reading to children is instantly recognised as a family routine – here performed by a civilised single mother. The overall segment of the ceremony casts young age mind-walking as a form of travel: as Dann (1989) has suggested, tourism temporarily reverts us to a child-like stage, unleashing our desires and resolving our inhibitions through pampering. The inclusion of a giant baby in the ceremonial sequence promotes Freudian language and human subjectivity, ego desires and id needs into projections of a collective global psyche. Lacan's reading of Freud suggested that the Cartesian self exists only through a system of symbolic functions that nevertheless act as the prerequisite for the social order (Lacan, 1998). The Olympic ceremony's tourist-like anomie invites audiences to become children indulging in aesthetic pleasures but their rebelliousness is built into a global symbolic order. Hence, toying with human imaginations through children's literature re-articulates the Olympic categorical imperative, even if audiences engage on stage with national allegories (British artistic creations).

But Rowling's presence on the Olympic stage also reminds us that images and their materialisation only serve to open up the mind to inner truths that set the soul in motion (Kandinsky, 1982, p. 21). Just as directors

DOI: 10.1057/9781137336323

and filmmakers, writers are mind-mappers and epistemological magicians communicating with their art-world structures and cosmologies (Ingold, 2000). The very motion from the craft of writing to the art of depicting and enacting are embedded in the much-loved stories selected for this segment. These stories were accompanied by famous sketches, drawings and paintings of considerable market value in contemporary cultural institutional contexts (for example, Winnie-the-Poo sketches at auction). Here we may discern how art and philanthropy may also counter the former's public conceptions as 'crypto-pornographic' (Atwood, 2002). To break the illusions of scale, artistic practices of giving in the form of philanthropy structurally correspond to the Olympic European economy of thought that places national achievements ('contributions to human development') on a par with the 'ancient' Athenian 'gift' (de Coubertin's 'Olympic spirit'). The exchange of the artistic *ánthropos* for a crafty *vrotí* unveils the artisanal origins of Boyle's Olympic tale.

'*Interlude*' allows for a transition to urban popular cultures retaining a distant relationship with the intimate domain of home. First we are directed to a series of British cinematic moments that appeal to global viewers – amongst them, *A Matter of Life and Death* (1946), *Gregory's Girl* (1981), *Kes* (1969), *Four Weddings and a Funeral* (1994) and *Mr Bean's Holiday* (2007). In this instance Boyle's cinematic literacy and professionalism create accessible 'mind maps' for the benefit of viewers: we too travel with him through time and space. Other global British brands such as Charlie Chaplin, Stan Laurel, James Bond and Harry Potter also frame cultural transitions from the post-war cultures of poverty and mourning to the glamour of betting, trickery, fast action and 'swords and sorcery'. Genre advertising aside, the running theme of movie magic is encapsulated through associations of comedy, acrobatic and intellectual skill, childhood experience and travel. Rowling's novels in particular work as a link between the films' varied mobilities: as allegories of social solidarity. Her stories enact a double journey: first, they explore the challenges of coming of age in an abusive family environment; and second, they encode the ways social groups come to act upon, shape and re-shape stifling structures of thought and living. Because the books belong to the *Bildungsroman* literature that focuses on character development (Bakhtin, 1986, pp. 20–59) they adhere to the ceremony's Aristotelian didactic qualities and its digital travel subtext. One may even argue that the *Harry Potter* literary (1997–2007) and cinematic (2001–11) series allegorise two opposing forms of organisation that we find in societies with

DOI: 10.1057/9781137336323

rigid and high authority on the one hand and mobility and stratification on the other. In *Harry Potter* the destructive forces of witchcraft are set against the civilising craft of sorcery, and used as mediums of social belonging, recognition and mobility. The seven movies are rife with understandings of *téchne* as an art speaking the language of nature, and as craft and technology mastering nature. But as the *Harry Potter* films are exercises in digital simulation, one may also recall Luhrmann's (1994) study of neo-paganism in western contexts as an interpretive development of emotions and experience that leads to rationalisation. The belief in cinematic simulacra and the hero's ethological maturation become one and the same on stage.

The themes of community belonging, family and suffering underscore Boyle's selection of the other cinematic legends. It is precisely these themes that provide understandable formulae of 'characters', at once human and irreducibly 'British'. Norbert Elias' (1996; 2006) theoretical investigations into the socio-genesis of rationalisation and psychogenesis of self-discipline are useful starting points in our examination of Olympic art worlds. Film characters project understandings of civilised habitus because their *acted* mannerisms establish firm boundaries between proximity, visibility and intimacy, and distance, invisibility and propriety (Elias, 1996, p. 2; Pickel, 2004, p. 4; Tzanelli, 2008a, p. 25). Originally habitus actualised versions of modernity, localised understandings of character that both safeguard and relativise tradition (Elias, 1996; Gallant, 2002). A by-product of identity narratives, character appears as a stable referent in time, an instant identifier of individuals as parts of a cultural whole (Ricoeur, 1993, p. 119), even though these individuals are subjects in flux. Habitus has practical and poetic qualities and hence partakes in the production of our humanity. Both the discourses of art history and sociology to which 'character studies' belong date back to the era of nation-building (see also Tanner, 2003, p. 1), but the staging of mannerisms in the theatre attested the creative artist's tendency to interpret dominant styles in ways that are both innovative and instantly recognisable by others. Rather than reiterate Mannheim's indecision (2003, p. 218) over the consciousness of character performance as an art style – an ambivalence replicated in Bourdieu's (1977 and 1998) theory of practice and his study of habitus – I view its post-modern mobilisation in Olympic art in terms of technopoesis.

In Olympic ceremonies directors are invited to project ethnic machinations, instantly recognised national typologies, *for* the benefit

DOI: 10.1057/9781137336323

of the host city/country *to* a global audience. Herzfeld (2006b) speaks of stereotypical projections of custom and habit as a form of 'practical Mediterraneanism'. Just as the generic 'practical Orientalism [...], the translation of hegemonic ideology into everyday practice so that it infiltrates the habitual spaces of ordinary experience' (Herzfeld, 1997, p. 96), practical Mediterraneanism is a philosophy of the margins inviting enterprise in contemporary industrial environments such as those of tourism. By analogy, 'marketable Occidentalisms' develop as philosophies of the centre to express a different form of marginalisation relating to the impenetrability of habitus. Boyle's marketable Occidentalism in the Olympic context is introduced through *Chariots of Fire* (1981, dir. Hugh Hudson), a story counterpoising the athletic character of a devout Scottish Christian (Eric Liddel) to that of a gifted Jewish sprinter (Harold Abrahams), who uses his prowess to confront prejudice (Opening Ceremony, 2012, pp. 28–9). The soundtrack music by Vangelis Papathanasiou that was used in this segment was performed by the famous London Symphony Orchestra (LSO) directed by the Liverpoodlian Sir Simon Rattle. The LSO's long association with various cinematic soundtracks (e.g. *Star Wars* and *Harry Potter*) shows once more how industrial networking guides contemporary Olympic ceremonies.

Boyle sidesteps associations of the soundtrack from *Chariots of Fire* with the cosmopolitan spirit of Olympic athletics, which promotes the orderly manipulation of embodied *hexis* and the production of civil habitus, in favour of a dialogic model of 'character-building' based on the ignominies of the humorous cultures of home (Tzanelli, 2012b). With the help of the camera and lighting the audience soon discovers that the versatile comedian Rowan Atkinson, globally celebrated for his impersonation of the silent character *Mr Bean* (2000, 2007) and his leading role in *Black Adder* (1982), is sitting with the orchestra, daydreaming that he runs on the movie's beach together with Hudson and Liddel, and contriving laugh-inducing ways to win the race. Just as the Queen's parachuting *debut*, such humorous notes are funny as wonders of what external viewers may perceive as cultural specificity when in fact all we confront is collaboratively contrived simulations (Baudrillard, 1988). The anthropology of tourism has taken many strides in this direction, proposing a dialogical model of identity-building through host-guest interactions (Maoz, 2006): whether our interlocutors are real, imaginary or distant, they enable us to comprehend ourselves. I understand specificity in terms of idiosyncrasy, the fusion (*krāsso*) of local idiom

DOI: 10.1057/9781137336323

(*krāsis* as temperament) that without global sharing (*syn* as together) would remain self-referential and secluded (*ídios* as the same) from global multi-sensory engagement. Bakhtin noted how laughter operates as cosmological supra-philosophy in folk traditions associated with feminine domains of reproduction and defecation – bodily mobilities in short (Murashov, 1997, p. 207). But foreign humour carries within the uncertainty of intention and behaviours controlled by those performing it – the Olympic *hosts*. Not only does humour adhere to the principles of modern civility, it also turns familiar domains into exotic products in intercultural communications.

Humorous or not, 'Interlude' is a form of pilgrimage to sites of imagination that Boyle both hooks and unhooks from cultural protocol through embodied forms of professional acting. Howard (2012, pp. 11–12) notes how the notion of modern pilgrimage that Turner and Turner propagated may be read as 'meta-social commentary' on our epoch and a search for vanishing virtues. In this schema the Heideggerian conception of *chrónos* as the mechanical and quantifiable time we read in clocks, the time of everyday life, is juxtaposed to sacred time (*kairós*), the site of myth in which spatio-temporal constrictions cease to define the subject's experience (Tzanelli, 2011, chapter 3). The ceremonies simulated character through selective borrowings from perceptions of British habitus in global cinematic domains. Idiosyncratic simulations of Britishness are thus transformed into global audio-visual commodities by the Olympics' artistic agents and actors. It is significant that Boyle selected Atkinson for this segment: the global success of *Mr Bean's Holiday* in which the character claims from a raffle ticket a trip to Cannes and proceeds to film the entirety of his travels on a video camera brings together various technopoetic tools (embodied acting, video camera, and filmed tourist landscapes) from the Olympic ceremony. Boyle uses the film's ending (Bean at the beach) to reiterate the *carnivalesque* structure of his cine-matic tourist play. As Shields (1991) has argued, the beach is the 'locus of an assemblage of [...] behaviours and patterns of interaction outside the norms of everyday behaviour' (1991, p. 75). Coupling a scene from one of twentieth century's cinematic masterpieces that speaks the *kairotic* language of Olympic work with the disorganised journey from a marketable comedy that embraces the temporality of tourist play challenges some hidden ideological hierarchies of civility that glorify Western habitus.

On the whole, the segment allows Boyle to revisit the original ideological convergence of travel, art and (Olympic) athleticism in

DOI: 10.1057/9781137336323

Eurocentric histories of mobility. The travel exploits of artists, students and colonial administrators to places Western empires recognised as Europe's civilisational birthplace (Rome, Greece and the Holy Lands) assisted in the production of a detached gaze as an ego-enhancing rite for the better-off (predominantly male) travellers (Dann, 1977; Tzanelli, 2010b). The shift from aristocratic leisure to middle-class conspicuous consumption during the eighteenth and nineteenth centuries dictated the accruement of symbolic capital abroad to display at home – a practice that continues to inform Western travel (Desforges, 2000). But the idea that artistic travellers would not travel between cultures to position the other as irremediably different (or inferior) to the self or that they would do so to this end (Said 1978) does not account for Boyle's pastiche. This encapsulates a pendulum-like movement from virtual, cinematic to embodied travel that both mimics and mocks at these Eurocentric ideologies. This pendulum-like mobility of satire is akin to a 'colonial mimicry' (Bhabha, 1994) that in the contexts of cultural industrial markets such as those of film and tourism can also be mobilised by the centre. The sequence Boyle uses from the *Chariots of Fire* was filmed on location in St Andrews's beach, Scotland. Scotland's peripheral geographical positioning in British discourses of identity complemented a romantic travel discourse early on: from the mid-eighteenth century the Scottish Highlands came to represent in British culture a form of civilised, tamed and 'controlled wilderness' (Mackenzie, 1997, p. 70). Today's Scottish tourist image draws upon these early narratives to produce a tourist gaze that is both romantic (seeking solace in the country's natural wilderness) and post-modern (seeking mass production, urban hubs and shopping malls) (MacCannell, 2012, p. 191). The segment's Scottish backdrop and Mr Bean as the foreground produce a place 'in play' (Sheller and Urry, 2004) that comes to life in cinema's 'technoromantic' apparatus (Coyne, 1999).

The ways in which intimate histories of nation-building joined contemporary leisure and tourist markets is carried through to the next segment (*'Frankie and June Say ... Thanks Tim'*) of the ceremony, which starts with glimpses into the weekend rituals of an ordinary family. This is played by volunteer performers. The insertion of family intimacies into global Olympic artscapes reiterates the observation that kinship networks regenerate in tourist milieus (Sontag, 1990; Larsen, 2005; Larsen et al., 2006). The house in the segment, a full-size replica of a modern British house, appeals to cultural fixities familiar to any native artist. A

DOI: 10.1057/9781137336323

product of both individual and collective manipulation (Connerton, 1989; Halbwachs, 1992), such memory objects allow the artist's inner journey make sense to others (Clifford, 1988, p. 167). The cinematic tourist family of the segment cuts across generational lines, with mum and dad staying at home to watch TV, the teenage son playing computer games and the teenage girl, June (Jasmine Breinburg) getting ready to go out dancing. Her encounter on tube with Frankie (Henrique Costa), a young man, follows through fast-action sequences the principles of the romantic cinematic genre that appeals to female viewers (Langford, 2005, p. 47). Here Boyle's time machine is symbolised by a regression to the age of melodrama – a genre that was deprecated as a woman's past time by an industry dominated by men (Gledhill, 1987; Neale, 2000, pp. 194–5). The casting is emblematic of a British multi-cultural utopia (both teenagers have an Afro-Caribbean appearance) that real politics challenge in a country with intensified border control and strict immigration policies. Policies of ethnic exclusivity are replaced by a narrative of youth, joy and leisure – three coordinates that defined black community contributions to Londonese sub-cultures of consumption and protest alike over the last half century (Gilroy 1993). The mixed profiles of the volunteers symbolise the socio-cultural hybridisations of a city that constantly trades cosmopolitan rootedness for lifestyle mobility. The insertion of ethnoscapal variables in the ceremonial artscape is constitutive of the cultural economies in mega-events such as that of the Olympics (Roche, 2000, chapter 7; Roche, 2002; Adey, 2010, p. 188). British migration memory pluralises national pasts, enabling the technological transposition of rooted landscapes in the stadium (Appadurai, 1981 and 1990).

These scenes do not reconstitute the 'authentic' working-class ethics of sub-cultural life, but stress instead the contemporary entrepreneurial dynamic of these enclaves, as well as young people's ambitions and desires for success (McRobbie, 2002; Snyder, 2012). This operates on a meta-level as a reminder that any emerging sub-cultural style joins the market and is consumed as a commodity (Hebdige, 1979). The fact that the segment unfolds in the public spaces of the London underground, the club and the street, reflects Bauman's (2000, p. 39) argument on the colonisation of the public realm by individualised intimacies and love stories. Frankie and June's love story, which unfolds through a series of clubs that play music from four successive decades (1960s–1990s) retains a technographic ethos that 'demythologizes the rhetoric of the electronic sublime' (Vannini et al., 2009, p. 473) in the tradition of comedies about

DOI: 10.1057/9781137336323

everyday life. Otherwise put, the story's mediation through cinematic genres and new social technologies amplifies its sublime quality, the feel of greatness and uniqueness of intimacy, but abstracts them as forms of utopia of the everyday. It is not coincidental that Boyle inserts in this musical and embodied sequel the London scientist Berners Lee, inventor of the Wold Wide Web, who is thanked by the soon-to-be couple in the segment's title for his digital gift. Not completely outside the European economy of thought, the digital gift revises the participatory potential of reciprocity by placing it in a global public sphere rather than in traditional kinship networks (Rheingold, 2000; Argyrou, 2013, forthcoming, chapter 1). Recurring tropes of such virtual utopianism in the ceremony suggest that social bonds can somehow be repaired 'through the migration of human interaction to online environment[s]' (Yar, 2012, p. 186).

Yet as Boyle the artist re-mediates the domesticity of family albums and memories through Internet artisanship, he also breaks away from the sexist histories of cinematic genres (Hand, 2012, p. 135, p. 164). The global phenomenon of social media creativity and networking (Boyd and Ellison, 2007) already foregrounds Frankie and June's flirting, which begins when he recovers her lost mobile phone en route to a club and ends with a social media invite back to the family house. The segment's network of mobility also includes a period Mini Cooper (car) that museumifies the histories of British adolescence to produce an Olympic spectacle at once familiar (for global aficionados of automobile technology) and familial (for British viewers), while also hinting at the urban background of the story's plot (Sheller and Urry 2000). Yet we may also note that the beginnings of the mobile world of the city hint at the rise of an individualist ethos that breaks away from family values. The world of automobilities has created temporariness in the structure of both 'public and personal value systems' that reflect contemporary transformations of intimate relationships (Harvey, 1999; Beck and Gernsheim, 1995). The story's kinaesthetic aspects (Kenrick H2O Sandy's choreographing of the huge group of volunteer teenagers [Opening Ceremony, 2012, p. 31]) also stressed expressiveness and freedom of acting, thus recreating the previous section's dialogics of familiarity and informality.

The music chosen for this segment is a fusion of older and new hits by famous artists, including The Who ('My generation'), Sex Pistols ('Pretty Vacant'), Queen ('Bohemian Rhapsody') Sugababes ('Push the Button') but also Underworld (Notably, 'Born Sleepy NUXX' figured in *Trainspotting*) and London-born Dizzee Rascal ('Bonkers', was number

DOI: 10.1057/9781137336323

one in the 2009 charts). Moving further away from the *kairotic* Olympic bubble, this musical medley foregrounds the replacement of one Queen (Head of the British State) with another (a pop band renowned for its musical pastiche). The enactment of the love story between clubs and dancing styles conceals the workings of British identity-building behind neo-tribal mobility (Maffesoli, 1996), the generation of an emotional bond between ostensibly disparate individuals. Malbon analyses clubbing as a form of *ecstasis* or in-betweeness of emotion and motion, 'a flux between identity and identification' (1999, p. 86) difficult to explain. The synergies of bodily motion, emotion and auditory mobility in this section promote a sort of affective pilgrimage as an alternative to that of patriotic reverence of national sites, ideals and icons (Bajc et al., 2007; Cavanaugh, 2008). All in all, Boyle's clubbing segment – a favourite topic he includes in his other cinematic work – could be read as a sort of ethnographic endeavour that de-mediates 'music in action' (DeNora, 2000) while simultaneously connecting urban sub-cultural scenes to the politics of belonging.

The well-known hymn '*Abide with Me*' that was played on the Titanic when it sank and reportedly became Mahatma Gandhi's favourite, frames the following section. Written by Henry Francis Lyte in 1847 on his deathbed, and sang at every FA Cup Final since 1927 and every League Challenge Cup Final since 1929 (Opening Ceremony 2012, p. 32), it signals a reversion to ceremonial thanatotourist rites. Fifty dancers including London-Bangladeshi choreographer Akram Khan who combines in his work European and Indian forms of dance, dramatised on stage the struggle between life and death through images of mortality such as dust and the setting sun. Although connections of such embodied artwork with human finitude are rooted in the European Neoplatonic theosophies of *vrotós*, the dancers' extensions to the universe in various poses projected a human aspiration to perfection reminiscent of the discourse of *ánthropos*. An analogous philosophy that values slow spiritual travel as an educational process (akin to *scholé*) generating peace, and its contemporary development into tourism (e.g. yoga tourism mobilities as meditation and the pursuit of embodied wellness) is also rooted in Hindu spirituality (Singh, 2012, pp. 217–20). Corresponding to musical styles that sprang out of various global mobilities in Britain (Gilroy, 1993; Adey, 2010, pp. 195–6), Khan's kinaesthetic artwork at once fixes and destabilises traditions. The assertion of individualised expression in communal ludic practices is, after all, at the heart of what Rojek (2010)

DOI: 10.1057/9781137336323

termed 'the labour of tourism'. Hence, just as the youth's clubbing communion from the previous scene, the dancers' embodied neo-pilgrimage in this segment outlines the principles of post-national *ecstasis*. Khan's previous collaborations with Orbit's designer, Anish Kapoor and Sydney 2000 artist Kylie Minogue also attest to his cosmopolitan identity as a world traveller (Hannerz, 1990 and 1996; Hannerz and Löfgren, 1994; Beck, 2000).

However, 'Abide with Me', which is sang by award-winning Zambian-Scottish artist Emeli Sandé, reflects the principles of slow mobilities. Not only has the hymn evolved into a collage of memory signs (Benjamin, 1973), it also articulates the 'metaphysics of presence', a utopian possibility of the gift of remembrance and the 'gift of thought' as a present (Derrida, 1994; Argyrou, 2013, forthcoming, chapter 3). In a gesture that mirrors Ranciére's (2011) model of spectatorship-as-action, visitors were invited to present images of loved ones who are no longer present 'in the flesh'. These photographs were then digitally projected onto the stadium screen to generate the atmosphere of individual-come-global remembrance. The hymn's association with sport suggests the transcendence of individualised memory in favour of a bigger 'absent presence' of war and suffering on which the Olympic spirit created new teleological possibilities: if war was death, athleticism was aspiration to perfection, hence the dialogical project of becoming *ánthropos* without forgetting past mistakes. Benjamin's (1992 [1968]) soteriological reflections on the eradication of remembrance from people's lives after the Great War, but also the sudden moral awakening this triggered in the face of total memory loss, might serve as background understandings and models for the creation of London 2012's digital platform for individual pasts. At the end of this collage's existential corridor we find Benjamin's elaborations on the 'anamnestic solidarity' (Lenhardt, 1975, p. 136) that war survivors ought to create with the dead, our moral debt to the past as a pre-condition for the preservation of democratic institutions (Fussell, 1975; Ricoeur, 1999; Misztal, 2003, p. 45; Tzanelli, 2007a, p. 254).

Overall, the segment's audio-visual travel appeals to the role of peace in fostering intercultural relations. Benjamin's anamnestic solidarity and the audiences' individual memories are sustained through 'emotional labour' (Hochschild, 1983), whereas the digital collage of absent persons de-territorialises and abstracts them as Olympic sacred time. Internet memory assumes an epic theatrical form akin to socialist montage, swinging between abstraction and specificity, theory and empiry

DOI: 10.1057/9781137336323

(Brecht, 1964 [1936]; Tomaselli, 2007, p. 83). This articulation comes to the fore as the segment connects to the introduction of the athletic teams in the stadium, with the Greek Parade first in the procession to honour the birthplace of the Olympics. The European economy of thought underscores the athletes' pilgrimage – to be sure, a rite of initiation (van Gennep, 1906) into Olympic sacred time. Despite the seriousness of the rite, its informal function for athletes as time of play, friendship-making and digital recording in individual cameras transforms the Olympic site into a dialogically constructed place 'in motion' (Bærenholdt et al., 2004; Haldrup and Larsen, 2010).The bifurcation of the event into publically accepted pilgrimage and privately performed yet globally broadcast consumption is constitutive of contemporary post-tourist trends that merge the everyday with the extraordinary and authenticity with simulation. This is also backed by the songs of the Parade, which include hits by older (Bee Gees, Pet Shop Boys and David Bowie) and newer (Adele) artists.

'*Bike A.M.*' celebrates the bicycle as part of everyday life but also the quintessential human-machine complex – a *tórnos*. The 75 symbolic 'dove bikes' or bike-bird hybrids were inspired by naturalist Louis Belle's dictum that cycling is the nearest approximation to the flight of birds: 'The airplane simply carries a man on its back like an obedient Pegasus; it gives him no wings of his [sic.] own' (Opening Ceremony 2012, p. 34). MacCannell explains that nature as an attraction may not have a scintilla of morality in and of itself, but tourists 'project highly moralistic frameworks on it'. But if nature is neither cruel nor innocent, it is 'said to be "wild" and "free"' (MacCannell, 2012, pp. 184–5). Borrowing once again from the Heideggerian anthropomorphing principles, the parable of this Olympic *tórnos* looks to the ancient athletic teams' homing dove, the bird released at the end of the Games to fly back to their cities carrying a message to their families so as to prepare a victor's welcome. Akin to artistic renditions of the Odyssean homecoming journey, this Olympic allegory articulates structural nostalgia for the long-lost (and always-already lost!) 'global human family', a restorative, if ultra-conservative, communitarian ethos we can experience outside transitory politics only in cinematic archplots (McKee, 1999, p. 4, pp. 64–7; Proust, 2002, p. 50; Gibbons, 2007, p. 2). The slow *kairotic* mobilities of the Olympics become intertwined with the fastness of the new technological era. This way we are led to believe that the ceremony's story of mass communication by Internet and mobile phones, as well as the postman and the paperboy

DOI: 10.1057/9781137336323

on their bikes, 'begins on the wings of a dove' (Opening Ceremony 2012, p. 34). The musical selection for this segment complements this discourse: Arctic Monkeys' 'I Bet You Look Good on the Dancefloor' (2005) and 'Come Together' (2006) enhance the feel of human automobility with their lyrical and auditory references to electronic and bodily technologies.

The economy of European thought is asserted in the section with the recognition that the modern bike was invented in Scotland by blacksmith Kirkpatrick Macmillan. The acknowledgment is placed in the Olympic ceremony's sacred time, which consciously propagates amicable fusions of art (acting, dancing and costumed performance) with craft (engineering). Significantly, Britain is a world champion in cycling, a sport combining strategy with speed and wellbeing with fair play. The ceremonial insertion of cycling simultaneously appeals to utopian ideas of peace and the intimacies of home – apart from the ancient connotations, biblical symbolisms of the dove from Noah's Ark carrying an olive branch as a sign of land are pervasive. By invoking the Olympic ideal of spiritual purity and motherly security, the cycling doves articulate a 'life politics' that counters the dictatorship of speed (Virilio, 2006) with a philosophy of slow travel. This allows the cyclists to enjoy the landscape away from the strains of post-modern consumerist imperatives (Rojek, 2010; Fullagar, 2012, pp. 99–101). Boyle's artistic narrative could be read as a 'crypto-feminist' intervention in the performativity of sports (Soper, 2008, pp. 5–6) if its aims were not openly aligned with the histories of the Olympic Games.

There is overt support for the aesthetic principles of an alternative hedonism in which slowness is both beautiful and beneficial (Haybron, 2008). Actors and spectators bear witness to a circular movement of leisure on stage, as the doves roam the 'velodrome' until one of them is literally and metaphorically lifted to the sky. The spectacle appeals to Serre's and Latour's (1995, p. 118) conception of angelic communication that immerses us in celestial informational fields and transmission systems. Along the same lines Krippendorf (1987) noted the centrality of our desire for domains of relaxation and peace in travel discourse. The god-like (yet un-godly) technology (mechanical and embodied) that organises the spectacle also supports the show's post-industrial archplot: on the ground we continue to follow human cyclical motion and on air we experience the ideals of mechanical motion. Ultimately, the human-bike complex joins the Rings in the mid-stratosphere of

DOI: 10.1057/9781137336323

our celestial world. Incidentally the playful conclusion reminds one of Boyle's *Sunshine*, a science fiction film about a crew on a mission to save the earth. Revising the soteriological content of previous segments that celebrate traditional rites of remembrance, this final note educates us on the ability of Olympism to symbolically rescue humanity.

'*Let the Games Begin*' introduces the two principal IOC (Dr Jacques Rogge, outgoing IOC President) and LOCOG (Lord Sebastian Coe, Chair of Games), dramatis personae of London 2012. Both men are examples of Olympic *tornadóroi*, with Coe as former gold medal Olympian (1980, 1984) and Rogge as yachtsman over three Olympics (1968, 1972 and 1976). Both men's speeches reiterated the ideals of hard work and sacrifice in the name of both fair competition and global glamour. The Aristotelian didactic principles continue to inform a globally televised, distant gaze that re-articulates athletic craft as *téchne* (Aristotle, 1996). The globalisation of this *téchne* implicates in the politics of marketing British authenticity and athletic 'heritage'. But this discourse stands outside this book's focus. Suffice it to note that the traditional raising of the British and Olympic flags as well as the rite of oath-taking fuses Olympic categorical and national allegorical imperatives (Tzanelli, 2010a). Through the participation of a selection of human rights agents, activists and athletes (Opening Ceremony 2012, p. 35), it emphasises the global community's passage to Olympic *kairós*. Notably, the participating countries' flags were placed across the path of an artificial green hill close to the Cauldron. On the top of the blooming hill a tree complemented the utopian message of the ceremony.

As a *motif*, the 'World Tree' appears both in Eastern and Western mythologies and religious doctrines as a symbol of Enlightenment and immemorial antiquity. But if we treat the human rights procession of the flag and the stadium's pastoral landscape as a unity then Boyle's artwork is not devoid of autobiographical notes (e.g. his Catholic origins): 'World Trees' framed sacrificial narratives as much as they popularised understandings of the sacred. Notably, the sacredness of these intermediary moments between a televised artistic event and the beginning of the Games culminated in the presentation of flashpoints from the 70-day long journey of the Olympic Torch in the country, beginning with its presence in the Greek Olympia. This mediatised pilgrim gaze is overdetermined by the economy of European thought, as it presents reciprocal cycles such as that of the Torch, which is ignited every four years in host cities, dies at the end of the event and regenerates in its

DOI: 10.1057/9781137336323

FIGURE 2.4   *The stadium's 'Olympic' Tree and Hill*
Source: Shimelle Lain/Flickr

DOI: 10.1057/9781137336323

birthplace (Buschman and Lennartz, 1996; Sinclair, 2000). This segment is part of the ceremony's 'mobility' archplot that explores Prometheus' 'original theft' of fire from the Olympic gods. The 'theft' of fire is an archaic alternative of human theft from the Edenic Garden, and as a world-transcending deed it puts practices of giving within the 'human family' in utopian clothes (Campbell, 2008, p. 35; Tzanelli, 2011, chapters 5 and 6). We can also note in passing that the archetypal tale of fire-theft as knowledge was carried on in the post-modern articulation of the Paralympic Closing Ceremony – incidentally, an event directed by Kim Gavin, who was involved in the closing event of the Olympic Games.

A short film presents the travel of the Flame in Britain as a miniature of this global economy of sharing: through glimpses at the passing of this gift among 8,000 Torchbearers – and though them, over 95 per cent of British land and its people – the Olympic *tórnos* becomes a post-modern watershed, both emotionally proximate and visually distant to us. We watch the Torch moving within London on the same day, from Hampton Court Palace by Thames and up the river on to City Hall, and from there at night lighting up the bridges and the city's water landmarks (MacCannell, 1989; Lau, 2011). The Flame's ceremonial movie illuminates London, the 'global city', as a natural and technological complex, a node of myth, heritage and post-industrial *landscape* inviting global *flânerie* (Urry, 1995; Urry and Larsen, 2011). The insertion of London into a net-work of Olympic neo-pilgrimages rooted in global memory enmeshes different phantasmagoric narratives from the imaginary European cen-tre of old (Athens) to contemporary Western media centres (Eade, 1992 and 2001; Sassen, 2001 and 2002). The transfer of the Flame by future sporting star Jade Bailey on a speedboat piloted by football legend David Beckham from Tower Bridge to the Olympic Park also presents London as a spatial labyrinth, an economy of sights-as-signs and hybrid com-plexes of drivers, travellers, cars and boats (Urry, 2004; Duval, 2007).

One of the greatest Olympians Sir Steve Redgrave carries the Flame into the stadium through an honour guard of 500 construction work-ers who helped create the biggest European Park ever from a derelict industrial site. This symbolic act re-articulates a hybrid complex of state and independent sponsors as post-modernity's community-builders, but places at the forefront their actual manual labour (Bauman, 1992; Tzanelli, 2011, chapter 4). The symbolism, reminiscent of modernist 'memory work' (Misztal, 2003, pp. 60–3), is a product of middle-class (professional) story-telling and its style resonates with other vernacular

DOI: 10.1057/9781137336323

arts (Heywood, 2004, p. 49; Earl, 2008, p. 412). Just as in the mechanics of 'Pandemonium', the tourist gaze this rite promotes, museumifies and beautifies abject cultures by stressing their contribution to British civility displays on the global stage. Whereas this arrangement places 'low culture' under neat taxonomic labelling of 'national characters', it unhooks the practice from its colonial origins (Bennett, 1995; Bal, 2003, p. 22). The sign economy of this human assemblage prioritises the idea of a dignified *Homo Faber*, the common worker as an athletic worker. The gaze is turned to the past but builds the country's present from a futural perspective in which the new incoming human potential already has a part to play. Thus, 260 of Britain's greatest Olympians share the Cauldron lighting moment, including six from the 1948 generation, but seven young Torchbearers ignite the Cauldron. The arrangement reflects the Flag procession from Beijing 2008 in which renowned representatives from the 1950s athletic generation partook (Tzanelli, 2010a, p. 229).

The Cauldron itself is a work of cosmopolitan articulation: its designer, Thomas Heatherwick, is ranked amongst Britain's most

FIGURE 2.5   *The Olympic Cauldron*
Source: Elizabeth Harkin/Flickr

DOI: 10.1057/9781137336323

creative thinkers. His other famous contributions – a blend of utility and cosmetics-orientated products – include the UK Pavilion at the Shanghai World Expo and London's new red double-decker bus (Opening Ceremony 2012, p. 36). His innovative urban contributions are examples of cutting-edge craftsmanship and his Olympic Torch is a material articulation of global athletic solidarity and peace. It consists of over 200 copper 'petals', each for a team that became a post-Olympic gift to their respective countries. The 'petals' are attached to the Cauldron's elegant long stems that are ignited to rise towards each other and converge to form a giant flame. Its dismantling after the event is paradigmatic of the workings of the Olympic *tórnos* and the transitory nature of its global community (The return of the project for the Paralympics serves as another reminder of the *tórnos*, binding the two events in recognition that the Paralympians are equal humans). As a natural allegory (a flower with a calendrical life cycle), the Cauldron presents Olympic technopoetics as the product of human memory (And here we may note that the Closing Paralympic ceremony articulated the seasonal cycle as a sort of human autopoetics). Just as Beijing 2008's embodied Flame of the closing ceremony (Tzanelli, 2010a, p. 232), London's Olympic Cauldron stood between nature and culture, the immobility of national origins and the mobility of post-modern cosmopolitan belonging (Conversi, 2001). If LOCOG's manifesto on the simultaneous provision of 'safe and green' Olympics incorporates some ecological concerns into the production of the host's civil image, the Cauldron's narrative is geared towards a human ecology of civility (Bateson, 1980; Tomaselli, 2007).

Historically, the Flame has been associated with European totalitarianism's strategic idealisation of the working body as an affective site. However, tourism theory, which stresses today how bodily affective mobilities produce collective understandings of wellbeing (Brennan, 2003, p. 70; Maffesoli, 1996, p. 36), proffers an alternative vision of the Olympic *tórnos* (see Dann and Parrinello, 2009 on the background). The 'working body' of the Olympic Flame is emotional rather than affective, a piece of art that stands for a clear epistemological programme that promotes utopian democracy and solidarity. The consciously articulated segment is cleverly dressed by Underworld's 'Caliban's Dream', a song especially written for the event sketching in its lyrics an earthly Olympic Eden. As a situational hymn, the song narrates a collective pilgrimage of sorts 'in the garden of the world', with 'a flame [that] arrives to guide us past the gold between the anvils of the stars'. The lyrics tailored the

DOI: 10.1057/9781137336323

Shakespearean hero from *The Tempest* to the needs of the ceremony, which depicts the Cauldron's 'affirming flame' and the hero's call to illuminate a path 'through the darkness'. It has been observed that Shakespeare's interest in visions, dreams and nightmares evoked theatrical performances 'provoking troubles' when they could become connected to wishful thinking (Szakolczai, 2012, p. 54). The Cauldron, Shakespeare and Underworld's song are thus displayed as tangible and intangible articulations of Britain's heritage industry for global audio-visual visitors at this particular moment in time and in this specific site. The Flame and every Olympic host's Cauldron have indeed been linked to political turbulence repeatedly due to their origins in the 1936 Olympics and Europe's disreputable heritage of racism. Although London's Olympiad has been remarkably peaceful, it still required some effort on the part of its artistic directors to revise these histories. The track writer of the song, Rick Smith explains:

> Frank [the writer] and Danny [the creative director of the opening ceremony] put forward beautiful, transcendental poems by people like WH Auden, Thomas Nash, Philip Larkin. They set the tone for Caliban's Dream. Very early on Danny encouraged me not to think in terms of "Eye of the Tiger" for the final stages; we weren't looking for anything testosterone-fuelled. Those poetic ideas that we had talked about initially just seemed so beautiful; we wanted to draw them in to the story of the torch. Karl [Hyde, Smith's partner in Underworld] spent a long time working with those words to make them flow, helping avoid all the possible clichés we could fall prey to. (Turner, 2 August 2012)

Transcending such histories' masculine stereotyping in this complex of design, music and narrative was not easy. Yet, Smith's words grant the artists' imaginative journey with a feminine tone that present (and revise) ideas of heritage and art alike as domains of gentility and intimacy (Bourdieu, 1977; Young, 1990; Herzfeld, 2005; Uteng and Cresswell, 2008). At the same time, the properties of electronic music in the song promote a type of perambulation appealing to stereotyped masculine mobilities. On the whole, the journey's association with the Flame's innate properties produces a blended gendered *flânerie* through time and space that frames the concluding section of the ceremony ('*And in the end...*').

The eruption of pyrotechnics in the stadium and around the Olympic Park may be a ceremonial convention, but the selective illumination of urban markers tells a story very specific to the host. Just as the

DOI: 10.1057/9781137336323

idiosyncrasy of humour, the artificial roaming in the sky points a God-like finger to the place's architectural wonders. The pyrotechnic illumination of the 115m-high ArchelorMittal Orbit, a permanent artistic legacy for the city that sits between the Stadium and the Aquatic Centre, is an example of London's new tourist gaze. The Orbit was designed by Kapoor and Cecil Balmond who picked the name to symbolise the extraordinary physical and emotional effort involved in the continuous creative and athletic journey of the Olympic synergies between mind and body (Opening Ceremony 2012, p. 37). Envisaging from the outset their creation as an 'orbit, [...] a continuous loop or continuous journey from the start to the finish' (ArchelorMittal Orbit, undated, p. 5) without crossroads or links, their work stands as the architectural equivalent of a Hollywood movie. The discourse of betterness is simultaneously cast as the legacy of Enlightenment in which 'being human' is grounded on continuous historical interpretation (Smith, 2007, p. 155) and a variation of global complexity, according to which a 'whole' laboriously emerges from constant re-arrangements of different conditions and in different spheres (Urry, 2003). Nikolas Serota, advisory panel member and director of the Tate Gallery, said that the Orbit provides 'the perfect answer to the question of how sport and art come together', and praised Mittal's 'really impressive piece of patronage' (ArchelorMittal Orbit, undated, p. 14).

Viewed from an institutional perspective, the project's patronage and endorsement (Chairman of the ArchelorMittal steel company Lakshmi Mittal, the London Development Agency, Mayor Boris Johnson) was bound to stir commentary and criticism. Indeed, the Orbit was both praised as a 'genuine eyecatcher' for the Olympics television coverage, a 'strange and enticing marriage' between the Eiffel Tower and the un-built early Soviet era Tatlin's Tower, with the biblical Tower of Babel as their 'best man' (Glancey, 1 April 2010), and compared to vanity projects such as Benito Mussolini's 'wedding cake', the Monument to Vittorio Emanuele II built in Rome, or the Neutrality Arch, a rotating golden statue erected by Turkmenistan's President Saparmurat Niyazov (Gourlay and Ruiz, 25 October 2009). Perhaps Kapoor's Asian roots allow for associations of his work with what critical theory considered as an Orientalisation of Asian cityscapes, which, when enclosed in cameras and polaroids, generate kaleidoscopic visions ultimately interfering with the ways we selectively appropriate 'the otherwise too complicated social world' (Hutnyk, 1996, p. 178). A *Guardian* online poll published on the

DOI: 10.1057/9781137336323

FIGURE 2.6   *London's controversial public art work, 'ArchelorMittal Orbit'*
Source: Sam Harvey/Flickr

DOI: 10.1057/9781137336323

official launch, posing the question 'Anish Kapoor's Olympic tower: a grand design?' recorded 38.6 per cent for 'Yes, it's a grand design' and 61.4 per cent for 'No, it's garbage' (*The Guardian Poll*, 31 March 2010). Both negative and positive evaluations by journalists appear to be over-determined by the economy of European memory that was bequeathed to wartime Olympiads (Tomlinson and Young, 2006). Similar to official statistics, polls often provide a partial picture, but in this particular case the question also seems to crack a door open to normative evaluations and the urgency to 'think in terms of exclusive canons of influence and stylistic descendancy [sic.]' (Harrington, 2004, p. 40). The Orbit seems to record disparate influences but its adherence to a dialogics of form is unforgivable when users/viewers are invited to evaluate it. In recent decades artists have become less hostile to commercial involvement in arts whereas their engagement with state agents does not necessarily reflect their personal political stance. There is no doubt that business interests and a concern over the urban host's global image may lead to various forms of spatial and architectural 'cleansing' during the Olympic Games (Herzfeld, 2006b), but the evolution of artistic creativity in terms of 'cultural entrepreneurship' is not the culprit for policy decisions (DiMaggio, 1982). An analysis of Olympic articulations needs further qualifying, or one risks joining the anti-globalisation movement.

The Orbit could be viewed as an exercise in *theoría*: the architectural design elevates the visitor's vision to the sky from two viewpoints or observation platforms that expose the Olympic Park in its entirety. As Inglis (2005, p. 98) explains, utilitarian public art stresses exposure, promoting an illumination of our physical environs and a stimulation of our senses (de la Fuente 2007, pp. 415–16). And yet, this piece of public art also attempts to challenge the Christian Augustinian utopia through the mechanical uplifting of the Olympic tourist (Jay, 1993; Szerszinsky and Urry, 2006). The collaboration of Turner Prize winner Kapoor, better known for his grand-scale public installations that blend art, sculpture and architecture, with Deputy Chairman of global engineering company Arup Balmoral, renowned for his blend of science, maths and architectural design, connects craft knowledge with artistic inspiration. The Orbit's iconic likeness to a DNA sequence but also its inspirational origins in another global icon, the Eiffel Tower, appear to traduce the conservative cult of memory that appeals to resentful nationalist competition: biology discourse reverts to culture but becomes detached from rooted images and struggles (Tzanelli, 2011, chapter 3). The Orbit does

DOI: 10.1057/9781137336323

not forgo the importance of the past as a 'scarce resource' (Appadurai, 1981) but uses it in novel hermeneutic chains: it becomes Stratford's vantage point for millions of visitors, who bring with them their own camera vision and proceed to attach their own meanings and experiences to the Olympic journey. We need remember that tourism 'involves an ongoing (re)construction of praxis and space in shared contexts' (Edensor, 2001, p. 60; Graburn, 2001, p. 151). There are many different performances and places dependent upon the performances that take place within them (Bærenholdt et al., 2004). So any established suggestions for the consumption of the Orbit by its 'auteurs' are revised on location by the visitors' sensory experiences (Veijola and Jokinen, 1994; Veijola and Valtonen, 2007; Cloke and Perkins, 1998; Crouch and Desforges, 2003; Tzanelli, 2010b). The Orbit is already unhooked from the Olympic heritage so as to operate as London's 'travel legacy' actualised in a creative pact between professional nomads.

The Orbit's metaphysics of mobility partake in the story of the Rings: at the end of the ceremony we connect via a filmed narrative to the Olympic balloon that is by now in the mid-stratosphere, from where we see our blue planet from afar. The celestial pilgrim, the cinematic tourist and the musical fan converge in these last two minutes. This felicitous merger is accompanied by Sir Paul McCartney's two landmark compositions, 'Hey Jude' and 'The End'. Like the projected appearance of Lennon's 'Imagine' after Frankie and June's love story, McCartney's rhythms sum the spirit of the 1960s counter-cultural revolution that defined the politics of generations closer to that of London 2012's directors, and continue to inspire youth (on this we may note again that Boyle's cinematic repertoire includes several references to youth rituals the 1960s bequeathed to contemporary pop culture). Lennon and McCartney's respective digital and embodied appearances in the show reiterate MacCannell's (1989) argument that musical journeys organise the tourist experience in ways other consumption rituals cannot achieve.

It has been observed by others that the pop figures of the 1960s counter-cultures both allowed for simulations of elite travel and enabled through their actual experiences as bohemian world-travellers new forms of 'global *communitas*' to happen on the screen, the stage and the radio (also Powell, 1988, p. 31; Tzanelli, 2011). The lyrics of some of these musical hits also produced new synaesthetic narratives of the lonely hero and heroine (Campbell, 2008) on a journey that concluded in popular culture's 'mediated centre': London. These 'journeys' draft a

DOI: 10.1057/9781137336323

superscript at two ends of the social spectrum (folk-working class and elite), allowing for the mediation of categories of subjectivity and self-identity through an aesthetic reflexivity that is instantly recognisable in Western tourist contexts (Beck et al., 1994; Urry, 1995, p. 141; Desforges, 2000, p. 929; Campbell, 2005). In today's global economy such mediations operate as forms of cultural capital in Bourdieusian terms also for the host city (Couldry, 2003a). Consider how the hypnotic effect of 'Jude's' 'na-na-na' brings together two dissimilar trends: one looks to thanatotourist paths (the Olympic heritage London projects from its particular viewpoint) whereas the other markets the British histories of musical mobilities (Robins, 2000, p. 196) and the futures of athletic fandom (Fraser and Brown, 2002; Stone et al., 2003; Street, 2004; Malfas et al., 2004). As a result, the synaesthetic capital of such merged tourist types in the ceremony appeals simultaneously to archaic superscripts and to contemporary mobility desires. The next chapter explains that such narrative fusions persisted to some extent even in the Closing Ceremony of London 2012.

DOI: 10.1057/9781137336323

3

The Concluding Show: Music and the Self-Creating Cycle

Abstract: *This chapter suggests that the Closing Ceremony produced a musical narrative for the host city that corresponded to the performances and stories of the opening event. The centrality of leisure, tourism and work in representations of London conformed to urban tropes of lifestyle mobilities with a global appeal. The ceremony's structural organisation and display of artists with personal connections in the Olympic industry and its conceptions of tourism and work crafted abstract ideas of kinship. Just as the Opening Ceremony's juxtapositions of everyday time to Olympic sacred time, the Closing Ceremony's artwork synthesised a post-modern spectacle based on the co-existence of slow and fast mobilities. These combinations defined London and Britain as a concrete place, a national 'topos' (=abstracted place) but also transnational 'space' in the Olympic temporal bubble.*

Tzanelli, Rodanthi. *Olympic Ceremonialism and The Performance of National Character: From London 2012 to Rio 2016.* Basingstoke: Palgrave Macmillan, 2013.
DOI: 10.1057/9781137336323.

DOI: 10.1057/9781137336323

3.1 'Family' illusions and musical travel

Dubbed 'A Symphony of British Music', the London 2012 closing ceremony was created by Kim Gavin, Es Devlin, Stephen Daldry, David Arnold and Mark Fisher. Featuring a number of globally renowned British music artists, it lasted around three hours and attracted about 23 million UK and 750 worldwide viewers (BBC Sport, 12 August 2012). Gavin acted as creative director and choreographer, Devlin as set designer, Daldry as executive producer, Arnold as musical director and Fisher as production designer. The overall show was described by Gavin as a 'fabulous emotional experience [...] an elegant mash-up of British music, a rich tapestry of British culture and life [...] something people [will] remember for years to come' (Sawer and Duffin, 12 August 2012). The participants included over 3,000 adult volunteers, 380 school children from the six original Host Boroughs, and 250 professionals (Official London 2012 Website, 2012, Closing Ceremony). Seconding Gavin, Devlin and Arnold declared that the show had to have a universal appeal while drawing on 'things British' – a comment that was echoed in director Daniela Thomas' promise that the handover ceremony to Rio would demonstrate Brazilian sophistication in pop hybridity (Bilton, 11 August 2012). The overall emphasis on music reiterated the power of art in the production of multiple mobilities and their co-existence with fixities of national 'essence'. However, for various reasons some British performers (The Rolling Stones, David Bowie, Sex Pistols, Kate Bush, The Libertines) declined to participate in the show and appeared only on the screen. The appearance of Spice Girls suggests a link to David Beckham's involvement in London 2012, but their consent was secured after negotiations. David Beckham and Spice Girls member Victoria Beckham figure prominently in mainstream press and in tabloids as the extraordinary common family, updating the cinematic melodrama with their separate career paths while also appealing to populist sentiment (see Rowe and Gilmore, 2009). The show was watched on television by over 750 million worldwide. It was regarded by the press as lacking 'top drawer' performers and a 'gasp inducing moment' (Petridis, 13 August 2013), 'more cacophonous than symphonic' but with 'the capacity to charm and amaze' (Williams, 13 August 2012), an hour-long advert for rock-show design with a Spice Girls 'exuberant tone' (Sutcliffe, 13 August 2012), full of the 'energy of British popular culture over the past few decades and the gaiety of our Olympic ceremonies' (Billington, 13 August

DOI: 10.1057/9781137336323

2012) and with 'touches of brilliance, beauty, and bewilderment' (Moir, 13 August 2012).

The artistic synergies behind the event sustain an articulation complex: Gavin trained at the Royal Ballet School, worked as a TV leading dancer and eventually turned his theatrical background towards choreography, stage direction and live events direction, including the Concert for Diana at Wembley Stadium in 2007 and the Help for Heroes concert at Twickenham Stadium in 2010 (BBC Entertainment and Arts, 13 August 2012). His involvement in charity events featuring children and his directorship of the closing Paralympic ceremony 'Festival of Flame' (8 September 2012) reflects the marketisation of reciprocity of the opening event of London 2012. Devlin is a multi-award winning international stage and costume designer, whose work crosses a range of genres, including opera, dance, film, theatre, TV and (pop, rock and rap) concerts. Her contribution to the arts is multiple, with sketching, painting and design as the basis of her menmothetical creativity. As she revealed in 2005, her artwork was originally based on family imagery and characters (The Stage, 30 September 2005). Daldry's curriculum compares to Boyle's: known as theatre and film director and producer, he was nominated for Best Director or Best Picture at the Academy Awards, for films focusing on memory and art such as *Billy Elliot* (2000), *The Hours* (2002), *The Reader* (2008) and *Extremely Loud and Incredibly Close* (2011) (see IMDB, Stephen Daldry, undated). Known for scoring five James Bond films, as well as *Stargate* (1994), *Independence Day* (1996), *Godzilla* (1998) and the television series *Little Britain* and *Sherlock*, Arnold is a fine example of synaesthetic travel – as he admits, a good director makes him 'see things and hear things' that otherwise he would not, enhancing his understanding 'of the emotional truth of a film' (Review Graveyard, 26 November 2010). Finally, as an architect, Fisher is known for his design of stage sets for Pink Floyd, The Rolling Stones, Tina Turner and U2, and for the 2012 Diamond Jubilee Concert. Arnold supports the Olympic caravan thesis, as he has designed opening and closing ceremonies for the Olympics (Torino 2006 and Beijing 2008) and the 2010 Asian Games, where A.R. Rahman's famous 'Jai Ho!' soundtrack from *Slumdog Millionaire* also figured as a celebration song (China.org.cn, undated). Their 2012 synergy and also their individual backgrounds and networks shed ample light on the selections of participating artists, the design of the show and also some localised similarities with previous events and with Boyle's artwork.

DOI: 10.1057/9781137336323

The 'axiom of amity' that was propagated by Fortes (1969) describes the production of leadership in industrial artistic networks, where monetary transactions also organise reciprocal connections and professional friendships. But in the context of the Olympic mega-event any 'borrowings' cannot remain hidden, so we have to assume that their performance involves the minimum degree of synergy between the relevant parties. By the same token, the involvement of various family members in the event appears as the outcome of professional connections and inferences rather than an antiquated arrangement in which women are traded for national glamour. The complexity of the phenomenon is inherent in the consumption of the finished product (Radin, 1996), which purports to project 'a bit of Britishness', however fragmented and post-modernised. This complexity is even more pronounced in the handover ceremony to Rio (2016), which was created by Cao Hamburger and Daniela Thomas, for reasons I explore in the final chapter. Here, I want to stress that real and fictional kinships travel on stage, the big stadium screen and in cosmopolitan imaginations (of artists and audiences alike). Much like Boyle's spectacle that fused understandings of national and transnational reciprocities, the closing event by Gavin, Devlin and peers developed as a synaesthetic rendition of banal tourist familiarities and everyday scenarios theory mostly associated with the democratisation of photography (Haldrup and Larsen, 2003; Larsen, 2005; Haldrup and Larsen, 2010, chapter 7; Urry and Larsen, 2011, pp. 208–10; Tzanelli, 2011, chapters 4 and 6). Much like Boyle's necessary abstraction of familiarity, it exoticised banal tourist spectacles for the benefit of a global audience (Prentice, 2004; Hannam and Knox, 2010, pp. 90–2).

The ceremony's focus on musical narrative re-introduces understandings of articulation (see chapter 1 in this book) as a definitive merger between 'nature' and 'culture' in art (but see also a discussion of Straw's model in Born and Hesmondhalgh, 2000, p. 31). Yet, we must also remember that symphonies *syn* (together) *fonoún* (*foní* as voice) – otherwise put, in the context of a spectacle they echo together in phenomenological terms: not only does music-making involve picturing ideas in one's mind (Carruthers, 1998), in mega-events it also involves embodied performance of music and lyrics or musical panoramas such as Damien Hirst's controversial stadium-wide Union Jack. Musical symphonies were consolidated as authentic artwork in the era of nation-building which introduced modernity's great *symfonía* (=agreement), the original social pact or contract of Enlightenment (Turner, 2006, p. 135; Tzanelli, 2008a, p. 185). Looking past Durkheim's or even Herder's conceptions

DOI: 10.1057/9781137336323

of the body as a social site (see Tzanelli, 2011, chapter 5) may obscure artistic symbolisations of the national body as a transient entity, a symbolic being 'in motion' or an angelic transmitter of image, texture, sound and word (Serres, 1995). There is a great deal of illusion involved in the closing ceremony, as its auditory and kinaesthetic performances are blended products of native volunteers and artistic communities, but as the Olympic narrative itself hinges on post-national ideals any such inconsistencies are passed in silence. Interestingly however, the priority on music, with image and embodied narratives seconding it, does not detract from the event's autopoetic integration into the allegorical narrative of the 'touring imagination'.

The directors of the ceremony denied in interviews that they subscribe to any grand narratives, but even mobility without closure operates as a narrative node. At an organisational level, showcasing some of Britain's best musical talent points to the model of the caravan because bands and musical groups roam the world for concerts. In this artistic context the replacement of nationalist or populist self-presentations with surreal or rationalist eclecticism based on technology might reflect the manipulation of exotic aesthetics of the Rio handover (see Born and Hesmondhalgh, 2000, pp. 15–16). It may be worth highlighting that, discursively, the idea of travel becomes elevated in the Closing Ceremony to an ideal through strategies of repetition that allow space for the creative closure of the event. Like all mobility discourses supported by technology, the idea of beginnings that meet ends has a teleological rationale, as it function is to contain imagination within a vision that is intimate – if open, in our case, to the world. Conforming to the principles of Bloch's utopianism, the Olympic artists' artwork projects the idea of the world as home, a non-existing domestic hearth that lies at the end of an autopoetic process in music, images and performance (also Thompson, 2012, pp. 38–9). The emancipated spectator of the ceremonies thus feels part of a global family in motion, even though (s)he is presented with the anticipated reality of what the artwork evokes (Ranciére, 2011, p 77). Let us then look at what this British 'symphony' had to offer.

3.2   Scene-by-scene

The introductory segment, '*Rush Hour*', featured a filmed countdown, a set of 'tourist glances' (Urry, 2001, p. 4 in Tzanelli 2010b, p. 30) showing

DOI: 10.1057/9781137336323

a number of locations around London that are globally recognised as mediated tourist markers. These sights-as-signs were symmetrically arranged so as to reflect the Opening Ceremony's countdown and markers. The cinematic structure echoed the mechanics of the *tórnos* once more, reminding audiences of the mega-event's mediated centre (London), as well as its situated role in the Olympic system of reciprocity. Such representations have become in today's global economy a form of cultural capital in the most conventional Bourdieusian fashion. As much as they partake in rituals that produce imaginary cultural centres (Couldry, 2003b), they also promote novel arrangements of modern fixities. So, when on the tenth chime of Big Ben the arena becomes transformed into a map of the Union Flag (Damien Hirst's artwork) complete with downsized replicas of Londonese landmarks such as the Big Ben, the London Eye, Battersea Power Station and the Gherkin, we are confronted with clusters of signs renowned both for their mobile and immobile nature. Part of banal nationalist rituals but also the discourse of the tourist souvenir, the image of the Flag valorises the national city-centre for the global 'tourist gaze' (Billig, 1995; Urry and Larsen, 2011).

As the stadium's 'land', the flag necessitates the presence of a landscape partly rooted in national memory and partly fluid due to its insertion in global networks of consumption (see Bauman, 2000 on fixities and fluidities in self-narration). Hirst's centrepiece was intended as a celebration of what Devlin termed 'the anarchy and diversity of British pop art, and by extension the energy and multiplicity of contemporary British culture'. The artists worked in unison on realising visually 'a centrifugal explosion of red, white and blue paint covering the stadium floor' that both echoed Coe's dream of an inclusive Games and 'the surge of national optimism that marked the advent of New Labour in 1997 [which] brought a revival of positive, if largely retro, references to the flag' (Devlin, 19 August 2012) but replicated neither. With 176 photographs and many graphic designers having spent three months creating super-high-resolution images of the artwork, the project entered the chronicles of British technopoesis (Hand and Sandywell, 2002) and tourist digitopia (Tzanelli, 1212a and 2012b) at the same time. The centrifugal vision of a national symbol propagated by Devlin leads outwards to the market and the global cultural fields (Bourdieu, 1977, p. 94; Adey, 2010, p. 142), reiterating her situational identity as an Olympic traveller in a disorganised capitalist plateau.

DOI: 10.1057/9781137336323

But if this introduction transposes audiences to the British-Olympic *kairotic* plane, where national symbols are revered, displayed and marketed to others, the set's and the 'road's' newspaper cut-out design with words from British literary figures such as Shakespeare, J.R.R. Tolkien and Poet Laurete Carol Ann Duffy form a leisurely preamble to a usual day in London. This in-betweeness of romanticised literary roaming and everyday automobilities asserted the event's travel-like liminality (Turner, 1969 and 1974), which is neither sacred nor ordinary, but an extraordinary rite of consumption, a neo-pilgrimage (Graburn, 1983; Tzanelli, 2010b; Tzanelli 2013: chapter 3). Anderson's (1991) thesis of nation-building through print-capitalism appears in the segment embodied in the country's imagined city-node, with humans ploughing its compressed scapes and its dissolving social millieus and lifeworlds (Albrow et al., 1997, p. 30; Dürrschmidt, 1997, pp. 56–8). Emeli Sandé, who first made her appearance in the Opening Ceremony, appeared on a truck and sang a verse and the chorus of 'Read All About It (Part III)', and the ceremony's choir Urban Voices Collective followed on with The Beatles' 'Because'. The match subscribes to musical autopoesis as a sort of 'social volition' (see Mannheim, 1936 [1968], pp. 292–309 in chapter 1): according to incorrect urban rumours the McCartney–Lennon composition had reversed Beethoven's famous 'Moonlight Sonata' (in C-sharp minor). Yet, despite some commonalities in chord between them (highlighted at the time by classically trained Yoko Ono), 'Because' is thoroughly unique.

By accepting the song's uniqueness we are allowed to investigate the segment's reiterations of two major clashes in modernity's technopoetic journey: one is technological and points to the ways classical symphonies were slowly replaced by popular compositions with electronic instruments ('Because' is emblematic of this shift); the second highlights a progressive merger between 'crafts' and human 'knowledgeability' as the early phase of artisanship production in post-national articulations of belonging (Giddens, 1984; Polanyi, 1966). Incidentally, the same clash guides the development of upper-class romantic travel to mass tourism in the apogee of European modernity, as we examined in Chapter 1. But the segment produces a mobility vortex: not only were The Beatles emblematic of the 1960s social movements, they were also 'four provincial, musically unschooled and self-taught Liverpoodlian youths' (Snopes.com, 27 April 2007) that turned distinctions of 'high' and 'low' artistic registers on their head (see also Herzfeld, 2005 on problematic

DOI: 10.1057/9781137336323

distinctions between 'high' and 'low' national cultures). It is stated that Lennon wrote 'Because' around Ono's ad hoc play of Beethoven's sonata as an interpretation of her 'backwards' performance. Art and craft fuse in this arrangement, as they do in Sandé's pop performance of 'Read All About It (III)', which in the context of the ceremony can be examined as an emotional rendition of the freedom of speech. The lyrics attest that their imagined maker has got the words 'to change a nation' but instead 'is biting its tongue'. It proceeds with the observation that this imaginary subject has already spent 'a lifetime stuck in silence' out of fear that (s)he will 'do something wrong'. Yet, Sandé concludes, if none hears the words, 'how are we gonna learn your song [?]'. Thereafter, the singer refocuses the lyrics action to herself, and in high vocal tone declares that she wants to sing, shout and even scream 'till the words dry out', place all this 'in all of the papers' because she has ceased to be afraid: 'they can read all about it', as the song's title reveals to audiences (MetroLyrics.com, undated).

It is significant that the lyrics suggest lack of articulation between a silent subject and the singer, who prompts them to 'speak up'. Setting aside London 2012's project of popular inclusivity, the song suggests a sort of criticism from an oppressed party that is not forthcoming until the silence reaches a crescendo (the chorus appears to 'voice' their viewpoint in very high strings). Whether we choose to examine it as an ambivalent rendition of the way the national public sphere works (or malfunctions) or as a contemporary update to 'Because's' background fusion between musical art and craft, its tone is both nostalgic and intimate – akin to the musical ambivalence of the cinematic melodrama that, interestingly, here is sang by a woman.

The subsequent merger of this performance with cellist Julian Loyd Weber and The Stomp follows on this narrative fusion: The Stomp performed on household items while suspended on the sculptures of the stadium's landmarks in the rhythms of Edgar's Salut d'Amour. The pop sequence is then matched by iconic articulations of the national centre: on top of Elizabeth Tower, Timothy Spall as Winston Churchill reprised Caliban's 'Be not afeard', allowing for the journey to come a full circle. As this historic personality is tied to Britain's heroic image in the context of a global conflict, its insertion into the network of Shakespearean references (Caliban) might function as an artistic attempt to repair the schism war introduced to the fabric of global solidarity (Szakolczai, 2012, pp. 50–1). Once more, the Opening Ceremony is matched with the beginning of the closing event in a recuperative manner, to restore utopian

DOI: 10.1057/9781137336323

family intimacies lost in London's urban palimpsest. The performance then accelerates, with more paper-cars entering the arena, horns overlaying the music, children and office workers dressed in newspaper print rushing to their destination, in a representation of London's rush hour and the audience's transition to (everyday) time. Only Churchill's command to stop reverts us to the sacred time of the Olympic Games, with the arrival of Prince Henry of Wales and Queen Elizabeth II with IOC President Jacques Rogge, the sound of the national anthem and the revelation of Hirst's artwork.

'Street Party' commences with Michael Caine's countdown from five from his famous impersonation in *The Italian Job* (1969). Actualising Olympic art's *diforic* potential, Caine's character development appeals simultaneously to native and global audiences: just as Mr Bean's frolics and antics, Charlie Croacker's (played in 1969 by Michael Caine) illegality exposes Britain's disreputable fictional Self to global audiences. Charlie Croacker is the stereotypical cockney sparrow con artist/thief 'who is savvy and street smart yet endearing and loveable [... and who] pokes metaphorical[ly] two fingers up to the establishment and relies on his own wits to survive the life he has chosen' (IMDB, 'Charlie Croacker, undated). This artistic intervention provides a critical reversal of the reliable law-abiding character that normally 'organizes the practices of a

FIGURE 3.1 *Damien Hirst's transformation of the Olympic stadium into a flag*
Source: Rob Fuller and EZTD Photography/BBC

DOI: 10.1057/9781137336323

society' (de Certeau, 1986, p. 24; Tzanelli, 2008a, p. 107). Caine-Croacker is the impersonation of the artistic *carnivalesque*, and in the *kairotic* conditions of the Olympic spectacle he can order an explosion that in real lifetime would alert LOCOG's anti-terrorist squads. So, when the Reliant Regal from *Only Fools and Horses* (possibly also a literal pun by reference to Croacker as the 'foolish thief') explodes with Del Boy and Rodney jumping out dressed as Batman and Robin, we (and the guests of honour) are guided away from the threat of 7 July 2005 (London bombings) and into popular culture. An amicable fusion of at least three different genres (superhero, crime and science fiction), the Batman films certainly present us with the autopoetic potential of artistic volition, because they make use of, exemplify, revise and give voice to wider assumptions, concerns and anxieties about social life, disorder and change (see Rafter, 2006). The practical aspects of Orientalism meet 'Occidental marketability': Caine-Croacker's legendary phrase 'You are only supposed to blow the bloody doors off!' pushes further philosophising about such risks to the background, by replacing it with that of confidence crime, befit for a persona that sprang from and was dramatised by the British 'illusion industry' (Tzanelli et al., 2005, p. 99). On this note the newspapers are removed from the vehicles on stage while Madness performs 'Our House'. This is the segment's overarching message: 'our' intimate domain is safe and populated with colourful street parties that resemble relevant segments of the Athens 2004 Opening Ceremony.

The rest of the segment includes a selection of other musical performances (Blur's 'Parklife', Pet Shop Boys' 'West End Girls', One Direction's 'What Makes you Beautiful', Ray Davies/The Kink's 'Waterloo Sunset') that symbolise Londonese social milieus in passing. Meanwhile, the centre of the arena is cleared for Spelbound 2010 winners of 'Britain's Got Talent', who perform gymnastics to The Beatles' 'A Day in the Life' as symbolisations of a commuter's work journey. 'Waterloo Sunset' further frames performing 'local school children', allowing the segment to cover both public and private British domains. It is Emeli Sandé's reprisal of 'Read All About It (Pt. III)' that will conclude the performance, accompanied by a screened montage of athletes crying in victory or defeat. The overall segment appears to play with proximity and distance, as nothing is as it seems in Britain's illusion industry: emotions are fabricated, concealed or spontaneously erupting through various pathways and by different mediations. The screen strips celebrities of their veneer to reveal their common humanity. The stark

DOI: 10.1057/9781137336323

ways in which Croacker's endearing intimacies give way to emotional voyeurism reiterates the omnipresence of gendered spectatorship and action (Friedberg, 1993 and 1995): cockney working-classness and uncontrolled eruptions on the stage and the screen are indeed 'Our (marketable) House', even though shared with other humans (athletes). The feel of this segment frames Britain's mediated centre as a crypto-musical node: 'cockney' is after all the literary legend of a human 'born under bow bells'.

'*One Day Like This*' signals the Parade of the Athletes which is led by the Greek team. Arnold's composition arranged the gathering up of the central cross of the Union Flag, with Great Britain at the rear. The athletes marched after volunteer marshals dressed in blue suits and bowler hats with light bulbs on top (a reference to a fictional 'British character' one also finds in the eight-minute handover segment to London in Beijing 2008 [Tzanelli, 2010a, pp. 233–4]) from various entrances while Elbow perform 'One Day Like This' and 'Open Arms' as a welcoming message. As the ramps of the Olympic Stadium-Flag fill and the national flags are moved closer to the Olympic Flame, the symbol of cosmopolitan unity, a reprise of some songs from the opening segment is played. The meta-narrative of reciprocity that framed the Opening Ceremony returns in the following segment, '*Here Comes the Sun*', which is foregrounded by 16 dhol performing drummers carrying 303 white boxes, one for every event in the Olympic Games. Succeeding this, a remix of Kate Bush's 'Running up That Hill (A Deal with God)' frames the arrangement of the boxes into a pyramid while video highlights from the Games' 16 days run on the stadium's giant screen. The song's lyrics articulate the ath-letic pilgrim's journey, a labour of love that is also resentment-inducing (God is called to swap places with the singer) (Adler, 1999; Tzanelli, 2011, chapter 1). Yet, the Olympic ceremony proceeds to replace the indifferent 'master of the universe' with human technologies and rites of recognition, including the medal-award ceremony (by IOC President Rogge, and International Association of Athletics Federation [IAAF] President Lamine Diack) for Men's Marathon and the presentation (by Katherine Grainger, Katie Taylor and another four athletes) of flowers to six Olympic volunteers representing their 70,000 peers. Pairing the international profile of men with the national of the volunteers appeals to the Olympic categorical imperative.

The musical centrepiece of the segment reiterates the subtext of the Olympic *tórnos* as leisure and as labour: George Harrison's composition

DOI: 10.1057/9781137336323

'Here Comes the Sun' belongs to The Beatles' 1969 album 'Abbey Road'. It was created under very difficult personal circumstances – at the time, Harrison was arrested for marijuana possession, had an operation and was forced to quit the band temporarily. For Harrison the song's creation coincided with the band's professionalisation, and his inspiration (in liaison with Eric Clapton) figured as a 'break' from the bureaucracies these changes triggered (Harrison, 1980, p. 144 in Wikipedia 'Here Comes the Sun', undated). Astronomer Carl Sagan wanted the song to be included on the *Voyager Golden Record* but EMI refused to release the rights and when the probes were launched in 1977 the song was not included (Sagan et al., 1978). The revolutionary spirit of the band; the song's hybrid instrumental technology (electric guitar, bass, cello, flute, handclaps); its exchange of offbeat metrical patterns with repeated harmonies; its folk influences (Pollack, 1999); and finally, its lyric's leisurely reference to the centre of the solar system, produce a cosmopolitan manifesto anchored on physical, metaphysical and emotional mobilities. Sagan's initial involvement in the song's promotion in scientific circles also casts it as an interplanetary journey – but of human leisurely labour, a revised form of musical *scholé*.

The second longest segment of the ceremony, '*A Symphony of British Music*', commences with Queen's 'Bohemian Rapsody' and with John Lennon's face on the big screen singing 'Imagine' together with the Choirs of Liverpool in the stadium. The recording of Emeli Sandé in vocals with Gavin Powell in piano is meaningful, as director Huw Tal explains in an interview: the artists were looking for a piece of music 'of epic proportions by an iconic British artist – and Imagine fits that brief perfectly'. Tal stresses how the lyrics of the song 'sum up the emotions we have all experienced over the last few weeks and it bookends the Games brilliantly – we opened with Paul McCartney and we close with John Lennon' (BBC, 12 August 2012). Lennon's 'iconic' composition is reminiscent of *doxologies*, articulations of the doxic reason (*logos*) in ecclesiastical motifs. The recognition of doxa (Bourdieu, 1977, pp. 76–7), the ordering of our social universe in instantly recognisable audiovisual formulae is pre-condition for another Bourdieusian paradox: their parading in global spheres as 'cultural capital'. This already signals a revolt against fixed cosmic orders, releasing 'what is ours' in the world as a consumption 'sign'. Lennon-the-British-angel and Lennon-the-popstar dissolve into interchangeable commodities, renditions of a mobile *ánthropos* in the Olympic context.

DOI: 10.1057/9781137336323

The 'symphony' extends to an audio-visual agreement of older and younger generations who together perform a thanatotourist perambulation. This thanatotourism turns imagined peripheries of the nation (queer, working class and young) into 'contested commodities' (Radin, 1996), granting them with a voice in the show – albeit a controlled, mediatised voice. The generation of a bust of Lennon's face/sculpture by the connection of white pieces resembles 'Memory Tower', the concluding section of the Beijing 2008 Closing Ceremony in which 369 acrobats generate a 'Flame' (Tzanelli, 2010a, p. 235), but also Athens 2004's 'Allegory', in which pieces of hanging sculpture come together to produce the modern Greek grand theme of historic European continuity (Tzanelli, 2008b, p. 502). Given the epistemic network of the event's principal creators, we may consider such similarities as manifestations of the 'axiom of amity', (Fortes, 1969) the generation of original artwork through creative repetition-borrowing. Here non-representational theory (e.g. mourning dead 'pop icons') meets romantic iconography, reminding us both of Butler's (1993) feminist performativity and of Thrift's (2008) post-religious materiality of glamour. Upon release of some balloons, George Michael sings his old hit 'Freedom!' and his new single 'White Light' – a move that raised some criticism as a form of self-promotion (Abramovitch, 14 August 2012). Urry and Larsen (2011) remind us that landscape representations are 'travelling objects, at once informational and material [that] become dynamic vehicles for the circulation of place through space and time'. Drawing on della Dora's (2007, p. 293) observations, they consider ways in which landscape-objects allow us to ' "pack the world in a box" and move about it, contributing to the shaping of knowledge of the world itself' (Urry and Larsen, 2011, pp. 110–1). The 303 'Olympic boxes' from the 'Here Comes the Sun' ceremonial segment and Lennon's 'marble face' in the following segment become technological transmissions of nationally rooted cultures, parts of yesteryear's working land-country (Williams, 1974) and today's global pop landscapes wrapped in cosmopolitan 'boxes'. The 'body' of the Olympic technology and the 'popular body' are the segment's consumed body. The Mods on scooters that enter the arena (a sub-cultural metaphor that corresponds to Boyle's relevant intervention in the opening event) carry Ricky Wilson to the stage where his band, The Kaiser Chiefs, sing The Who's 'Pinball Wizard'. The Kaiser Chiefs are a band from Leeds and their presence in the ceremony suggests once more georgraphic-cultural inclusion of Northern artscenes in the show. This act works on the principles of dexterity as a

DOI: 10.1057/9781137336323

civilisational marker: Pete Townsend wrote the lyrics of this song from the standpoint of a pinball champion, called 'Local Lad' in the Tommy libretto book, who is astounded by the skills of the opera's eponymous main character, Tommy Walk. This musical encounter, between operatic (designated as 'high') and pop (designated as 'low') registers, also adheres to the double principles of *tórnos* – at once leisurely and laboured.

Hebdige's (1979) take on sub-culture as meaningful style that we encountered in the Opening Ceremony appears to frame the role of craft in this segment: songs and images of David Bowie (another highly versatile, idiosyncratic artist who blends in his work embodied craft, vocal art and play) are used while the Mod scooters circle the arena. Bowie's hybrid career, which is marked by stylistic inconsistencies, works as a link to the next section (see NNB-David Bowie, undated). This section develops the ceremony's marketable Occidentalism: eight billboards with artwork of models arrive on the stadium but are soon replaced with several famous models from the British fashion industry walking in catwalk style and dressed in garment designed by famous designers. The performance, which was widely criticised in the press for its inclusion of some names (e.g. Kate Moss and Naomi Campbell) with suspect affiliations (Faulkner, 13 August 2012; Vicat-Brown, 13 September 2012), is emblematic of a 'cosmetic' cosmopolitan discourse that mobilises surfaces and glamour (Nederveen Pieterse, 2006b). It symbolises the ways new knowledge economies revise traditional frameworks of belonging along geospatial movement for work, everyday rhythms and hopes and urban mobilities (Freudendal-Pedersen, 2009). Showcasing their bodies, these feminine model-tourists easily come under fire for personal misbehaving. Their performance is also reminiscent of post-modern adulations and 'speed cultures' of the city we encounter in urban filmographies (Savelli, 2009, p. 151). The city-system and the city-museum converge in this segment that consolidates classification registers of human types 'in motion'.

We have already moved to post-modern planes defined by pastiche and deconstruction that is fronted by feminine icons: this is signalled by Annie Lennox's Gothic performance of 'Little Bird' on a black wooden boat but also an artistic symphony (by Richard Jones of The Feeling, Nick Mason of Pink Floyd and Mike Rutherford of Genesis and Mike and the Mechanics singing Floyd's 'Wish You Were Here') and some acrobatics (a performer shaking hands with a mannequin on tightrope as a reference to Floyd's 1975 album cover). If Boyle's rendition of pastiche adheres to Western cinematic tropes, this segment's equivalent is exemplary of the

DOI: 10.1057/9781137336323

new aesthetic forms that circulate in global musical imaginations where referentiality gives way to simulacra (Born and Hesmondhalgh, 2000, p. 28). The grotesque effect of this arrangement resembles the design of the Paralympic Closing Ceremony in which director Kim Gavin toyed with forms reminiscent of films such as *Mad Max*. The predominance of mobile and automobile vehicles in the Closing Ceremony of the Olympiad appeals to future scenarios of apocalyptic scarcity in natural resources often associated with critical debates on environmentalism (see Dennis and Urry, 2009). In this respect, ceremonial articulations of the host as a potentially 'dying' culture connect to the actual urban background of London 2012 and the concerns of relevant policymakers. However, the techno-scientific dystopianism of popular fiction is diluted in the Olympic ceremony through a deconstruction of ordered tropes of belonging. The artistic show seems to draw upon conceptions of the body as social allegory: wrecked bodies of ships, feminine bodies adorned with Gothic paraphernalia, pop bands dressed in unconventional cloth-ing. Bakhtin (1968, p. 26) reminds us that the upper body is traditionally regarded as the impenetrable site of logic and the noble senses and stere-otyped as male, whereas the lower body is vulnerable to invasion and thus constitutes the site of the feminine grotesque. Contemporary media discourses use such tropes to reconcile exotic 'vulgarity' with European artistic refinement, eventually embedding both in the commercial milieus of tourism (Spooner, 1986, pp. 222–3). Shocking, amusing and repulsing, the sequence contrasts with the ideal of Olympic harmony. Unsurprisingly then, this is followed by a bus carrying Russell Brand that mimics 'I Am a Walrus' and Fatboy Slim that plays 'Right Here, Right Now' and 'Rockafeller Skank' as the bus transforms into a giant inflatable octopus. The segment ends with three convertible Rolls-Royce Phantom Drophead Coupés with artists on their roofs (Jessie J. singing 'Price Tag', Tinie Tempah singing 'Written in the Stars' and Taio Cruz singing 'Dynamite'). After a full lap of the arena, all three cars combine and the stars sing Bee Gees retro hit 'You Should be Dancing'.

The prevalence of automobile in the ceremony borders on fetishism for good reasons: performers exaggerate late modern practices of stardom individuation in the context of an aesthetic reflexivity (Giddens, 1990 and 1991; Beck et al., 1994) that breaks away from the original Olympic ethics. As Urry notes (2007: 120) 'the car system has reorganized time and space, "unbundling" territorialities of home, work, business and leisure that were historically closely integrated'. Assertions of individual glamour

DOI: 10.1057/9781137336323

in London's artistically projected cityscape on 'technological move' herald the neo-liberal pantheon of global markets, not the Olympic pantheon of 'game-making', which is regulated by volunteering and solidarity. The black cabs with LED lights that enter the stage carrying Spice Girls speak the language of a market that transforms centrifugality into a feminine trait. In fact, the band performs a series of some of their hits that feminise centrifugal aspiration to celebrity and glamour ('Wannabe', 'Spice Up Your Life'). Incidentally, their appearance is followed by Beady Eye's 'Wonderwall' and by 'Mr. Blue Sky' by Electric Light Orchestra to celebrate British invention. With the subsequent appearance of Eric Idle out of a cannonball, who sings 'Always Look at the Bright Side of Life' in the company of nuns on roller-skaters, Roman soldiers and Punjab bangra musicians and dancers, we come full circle: the British grotesque is feminine, idiosyncratically funny and marketable. Muse's performance of London 2012's official song 'Survival' and a half projected (Freddie Mercury), half-embodied (Brian May and Roger Taylor) performance of 'We Will Rock You' also stresses the queerness (stereotypically seen as grotesque and subaltern [follow Weeks, 1977]) of British popular scene. The sequence is reminiscent of London's marketable Occidentalist ethos – a performative habitus celebrated with the eruption of fireworks.

The handover ceremony to Rio that follows the segment partakes in this discourse in a thoroughly Brazilian fashion. The closing speeches by Rogge and Coe were followed by an equally dramatic extinguishing of the Flame in a separate section that brought the Games to a close at midnight. The arms of the Cauldron were part-lowered and as the copper petals' fire dies out more fireworks set off behind it and Take That's 'Rule the World' sentimentalises with its lyrics the 'Spirit of the Flame', pleading 'don't leave me now' and 'don't fade away'. Darcey Bussell, who descends from the top of the stadium in the guise of a phoenix to dance the 'spirit of the flame' with four ballerinas, simultaneously also suggests a feminisation of art. It seems that, every time the performance relates to old Olympic formulas and protocols, traditional separations of art from technology return to vilify wider divisions of labour tasks that demote artistic work to unessential or peripheral labour performed by women or neurotic men (Molotch, 2004), reserving technological labour for those who conform to normative models of hegemonic masculinity (Connell, 1987 and 1995).

Such parochial paradigms of mobility are slowly being revised in institutional contexts. But this debate exceeds the focus of this study. Here I

DOI: 10.1057/9781137336323

FIGURE 3.2   *A Phoenix rising from the Olympic ashes*
Source: Rob Fuller and EZTD Photography/BBC

prefer to stress how ceremonial depictions of the Flame as a 'hermaph-
rodite' beautifully lingered in the air above the Cauldron in the shape
of a flaming phoenix (Rees, 13 August 2012). Historically 'the phoenix
flame' served as an allegory of the resurrected spirit of subaltern nation-
hoods such as the Irish and the Greek, producing in the latter case also a
pro-Olympic statement for the survival of antiquity in national modernity (Tzanelli, 2008a, p. 34; Tzanelli 2008b, pp. 429–34). The 'phoenix's
flame', which regenerates every four years in a different place, but always
in human space, is the Promethean promise of eternity. But the flaming
Phoenix's uplifting over the Olympic Cauldron also echoes the tragedy
of democracy, 'where the god is beheld crucified in the catastrophes not
of the great houses only but of every common home' (Campbell, 2008,
p. 27). Death is in this instance something that unites humanity in
mourning and celebration. This is akin to the familiar Christological arc
that presents crucifixion and *káthodos* (descending) to the Underworld
as the promise of *ánodos* (upcoming) after the purging of our sins (*pur-
gatorio* also means *catharsis*). The two ceremonies' oscillation between
comedy and tragedy is thus humanity's great escape from the inevitability
of death *and* oblivion. The athletic hero is the segment's absent presence,
as an abstracted human who achieves a domestic 'microcosmic' victory
(medal-winning) before (s)he joins Olympic artwork's 'macrocosmic

DOI: 10.1057/9781137336323

triumph' (Ibid., 37). This theoretical mobility marks the passage from physical to moral action – the very definition of the IOC's categorical imperative. Thus, the Closing Ceremony's artistic journey also suggests hermeneutic circles beyond the domains of nationhood, in a global media village. The technopoetic intervention also connects to Gavin's Paralympic 'Festival of Light' that invoked noetic sites of global memory (cf. Nora, 1989): the 'original theft' of knowledge. Foregrounding the Olympic Rings, the Phoenix and the Cauldron bring together allegorical and Olympic imperatives while also toying with the grammar of the global market – how else did we jump from firework celebrations of Britain's marketable Occidentalism to a neo-pilgrimage of the Flame? A rather banal answer is provided by the Rio 2016 performers: not only did Brazilian artwork capitalise on the country's thanatotourist potential – an enterprise necessitating solitary amnesia, forgetfulness of the pasts of slavery and racial segregation – it also nicely matched the closing act of the main ceremony, in which The Who performed songs such as 'My Generation' as a backdrop to image montages from the Games and firework display. Something was celebrated in those eight minutes of the handover – but what?

DOI: 10.1057/9781137336323

4

Struggling with the Other: Embodied Styles as Tourist Articulation

Abstract: *This chapter examines the Handover Ceremony to Rio (2016) as a marketable revision of Brazil's colonial history that leads to the artistic display of ideal types and ethnic characters for global audiences. The backgrounds of Brazilian political revolt and oppression contributed to repetitions of culturally situated patterns of work as mere consumable narratives. Rio's artistic narrative was based on exotic marginalities (black 'racial types') that correspond to Brazil's vulnerable or uncouth lifestyles and characters (samba dancers, capoeira and Candomblé performers, 'bad men' and glamorous white women). The ceremony's articulation enmeshed all these types and styles into Rio's self-presentation as a tourist 'topos' that was born out of past mobilities of humans, customs and embodied narratives of labour.*

Tzanelli, Rodanthi. *Olympic Ceremonialism and The Performance of National Character: From London 2012 to Rio 2016*. Basingstoke: Palgrave Macmillan, 2013.
DOI: 10.1057/9781137336323.

DOI: 10.1057/9781137336323

4.1   Brazilian articulations: anthropophagy and *cathexis*

Brazil figures as a quintessentially exotic topos in European imaginaries of consumption: a former colony, a destination for migrant groups from Europe, Africa and the Americas, and a cultural 'melting pot', it is as hard to fix and define as it is to physically traverse. For centuries debated as an extension of the Darwinian terra nova, but also as an anthropological paradise, its transition to the era of mobility is an as-yet incomplete project. In many respects, Brazilian developmental prerogatives work as an obstacle in the production of a coherent artistic self-narration. But this 'weakness' also became the Olympic handover's strongest point, because it allowed for the creation of a dialogical utopia on stage. In this utopia, clashes of folk and subaltern with the high cultures inspired by the country's European past are resolved for the global tourist gaze in ways that are impossible in realist contexts (Moreiras, 1999, p. 133 and 2001, p. 252; Popovitch, 2011, pp. 37–9). On the realist scene modern Brazilian governance ensured the country's much-debated political transition from a 25-year military dictatorship (1964–89) to a neo-liberal democracy. This transition defined institutional organisation in three interconnected spaces: the military, the political and the bureaucratic (Nervo Codato, 2006). Brazil's colonial experience generated links between fearful cannibalist stereotyping and another sort of visual 'anthropophagy', the voracious consumption of human polyvocality. The latter's mission is reminiscent of the Borgesian tales of Western travellers who fall in love with the land and become natives, reversing the colonial amnesias we know only too well, by turning them into extensions of self-betterment (Borges, 1998; Tzanelli, 2008a, p. 178).

Borgesian fables already craft Brazil's developmental archplot, according to which native populations and Western free minds are devoured by military *getulismo* (=authoritarianism). Atlantic pathways such as that of post-colonial Brazil are good examples of the ways individual societies were woven into complex relations of global interdependence (Benjamin, 2009). Therborn (1995) and Nederveen Pieterse (2009) provide useful generic starting points here with their argument that variations in modern societies are the product of different paths 'in and through modernity' or 'multiple modernities'. In federalised Brazil's case, uneven transitions to democracy harboured a fragmented governance model in which administrative maladjustment and the overall ill-defined

DOI: 10.1057/9781137336323

functional boundaries between branches of the state became sources of infinite conflict, prompting bureaucrats to strengthen their ties with external 'allies' and 'clients'. As a result, regional policies favoured disorganised capitalism, allowing for continuities between (liberal) ideological discourse and (crypto-authoritarian) political practice, as well as a 'deficit in citizenship' (Nervo Cordato, 2006). At the same time the onset of industrialisation and increased urbanisation transposed in big cities old citizenship struggles originating in the age of slavery (Krishna and Nederveen Pieterse, 2009). The strong tradition of Brazilian social movements was inextricably associated with the designated cradle of *Brasilidade* (Brazilianness) in the Northeast – a region considered both 'underdeveloped' and multi-cultural within the nation-state. Their historic connection to the Church fostered a philanthropic ethic that placed emphasis on the protection of vulnerable groups, sustainable development of international networks, human rights and the environment (Barreira, 2011, p. 153) and was geared towards ideological alliances between Christianity and activist Marxism (Garrison, 1996, p. 250). But the imported Cartesian cogito of European Christianity did not sit well with the native unity of mind and body that defined especially Afro-Brazilian ontologies. Because 'being in the world' connects to knowledge pathways (epistemologies), from the outset Brazilian self-presentations split between a (racialised) urgency to polish and whitewash civil surfaces and the agential project of acknowledging the country's ethno-cultural polyvocality and cultural-ontological unity in its own right. Let us not forget that *ethnic embodiment* is regarded as a form of primitive orality that can be inscribed upon, manipulated and re-invented by the skilled.

As imaginary travels, Olympic ceremonies retain the memory of such anthropophagies in that their mission is to reiterate 'Man's' abstract properties but also visions of 'disposable heritage' that might eventually produce new cosmopolitan topographies (hooks, 1992; Cohen, 1995; Nederveen Pieterse and Parekh, 2009). 'Cannibalism' rested upon European colonial inceptions of aboriginal culture that were promoted by convergences of the routes of New World explorers, political relocations of First World slavery and cultural mobility of alien custom. This is how the European imaginary of self-consumption would first transform into an exotic ethos that stood outside civilised humanity and later into travel brochures on adventurous New World holidays addressed to travellers looking for leaps to liminal spaces of experience (Hall, 1992,

DOI: 10.1057/9781137336323

p. 310; Hall, 1996; Massey, 1993 and 1994; Pattullo, 1996; Sheller, 2000; McClintock, 1995; Tzanelli, 2011, pp. 8–9). Rio's handover show focuses on this transitional phase in which the abject Brazilian body of subaltern dancers choreographs – literally and metaphorically – Brazil's national body as a contested commodity (Radin, 1996). This is so because the city's artistic pool is supported by past and present migrant mobilities from Europe and Africa with traditions of embodied labour. However disadvantaged (if not because of their disadvantaged social standing), such human resources, institutionally recognised as subjects akin to Bauman's 'vagabonds', hardly lose the character of the journeyman and woman, but never the ability and will to strike (Deleuze and Guattari, 1988). Splits between the nomad, the artisan and the (state) architect sustain the emancipatory power of labour circuits, and produce the model of the *tórnos* (as ceremonial tourism) of this chapter.

Although I recognise artistic independence from the bureaucratic realm (see previous chapters), I do not seek to fully disconnect artistic concerns from the cultural contexts in which they are born. Artistic indifference to context is never a-political, on the contrary, it constitutes a unique politics with a traumatic record in Brazil. Connell (1995) reminds us that gender as a social category interacts with race, class and sexuality and he uses the ancient Greek term *cathexis* to describe the gendered character of sexual desire and the practices that shape that desire in the 'gender order'. His analysis draws upon Freud's mechanical conceptions of *Bezeichnung* – a German translation of *cathexis* that refers to the functioning of psychosexual energies and the subject's investment of libido (Freud, 1982, pp. 381–2; Wain, 1998, pp. 125–6). Connell's observation might support another post-Freudian innovation in intersectional theory that certainly applies to Brazilian artistic creativity. The applicability of 'lashing out' mechanisms on group behaviour is as old as the project of critical theory but here I am more interested in *la longue dureé* disconnections between politics and art that create and recreate economies of signs and the European economy of thought. The Brazilian artistic scenes of samba, carnival and capoeira are haunted by the memory of political oppression but when performances begin to travel the world 'artistic caravans' become pre-occupied with the translatability of such particular national *leitmotifs* rather than overt productions of political statements. 'Travel' itself is *cathexis*: it works as a liberation from the past, opening up new entrepreneurial horizons. Academically, my argument re-examines Sarlo's (1994) early claim that value-neutral approaches to art are poorly

DOI: 10.1057/9781137336323

equipped to confront the challenges of neo-liberal organisation of cultural production but contests her perplexing exaggeration of ontological distinctions between art and other cultural forms (Sarlo, 1999). All three Olympic ceremonies in 2012 attempted to restore this schism by combinations of embodied and audio-visual means, thus placing emphasis on aesthetic experience in artistic creativity and discarding rigid versions of the formalist paradigm.

One might argue that ceremonially, Connell's Freudian *cathexis* functions as a form of Aristotelian *catharsis* for knowing insiders and performers. The traumatic process of political autopoesis (of memory, revolt and re-instatement of oppression) is transcended at the ideational level as artistic autopoesis, the repetition of culturally situated *leitmotifs* and patterns (embodied, emotional and auditory) as mere (consumable) 'signs'. As the anthropophagous project is placed in the hands of privileged natives (artistic directors), it becomes a valorisation vehicle: exotic interiorities and marginalities that serve as vulnerable or uncouth modes of social being (see Mannheim, 2003 on 'social volition') but are accommodated into non-paternalistic cultural self-presentations, provide the archplots of artistic performance. For this reason the structures and forms of the handover ceremony were borrowed from everyday life rituals of extraordinary cosmological proportions. This ritual abstracts masculine and feminine habitus and produces movie-like simulacra of sociality. Geertz's discussion of Balinese cockfight rituals as both amplifications of the 'narcissistic male ego' (Geertz, 1973, p. 419) and grand cosmological statements social institutions use in political discourse is a useful starting point (Smith, 2008). To distance themselves from harmful associations with Brazil's authoritarian past while espousing cosmological statements that make sense to Brazilian outsiders and global audiences, Brazil's artistic directors had to struggle with 'otherness' within the nation, and to include in their narrative domesticated forms of abject but marketable socialities and intimacies. In this conjunction the poetics of the nation-state (as in Herzfeld 2005) and artistic poetics (as in Wolff, 1984 and 1987) commenced a dialogue replete with conflict and revisions. In what follows I argue that this troublesome Brazilian 'dialogue' rested its case on the bureaucratisation of performance genres (samba, capoeira) that framed national self-narration within the nation's culturally fragmented domain and outside it as tourist commodities.

Where would this leave the artist, who does not necessarily endorse this bureaucratic ethos? A brutal but pertinent metaphor would point to

DOI: 10.1057/9781137336323

the murder of such bureaucratic tropes and the re-birth of past genres as cosmopolitan artwork that mocks bureaucracy from a safe distance – on stage. Of course, a subtle satire of social mores characterised the opening and closing ceremonies of the 2012 Olympiad that developed in a different socio-cultural context. In addition to satire, the 2012 handover spectacle used Brazilian genres framed specifically by ideas of (masculine) violence and (feminine) eroticism to enact a critical thanatotourist journey based on pastiche and embodied mobilities. Freud's (2002) and Marcuse's (1955) pairing of *eros* with *thanatos* and Dann and Seaton's (2001) examination of slavery as 'dissonant heritage' in global tourisms are pivotal for an examination of the teleology of artistic-tourist desire here. A striking homology develops between the migration of Brazilian artistic communities outside the national domain and the global mobility of subaltern, lumpen genres outside Brazilian bureaucratic discourse that thrives on emotional withdrawal and performative irony (Sarlo, 1988 in Popovitch, 2011, p. 42; Nietzsche, 1996; Scheler, 2003; Bowles, 2003; Tzanelli, 2011, chapter 6). The political conditions in the country have altered significantly over the last decade, but the historical phantom of violence still looms large, constantly re-activating mechanisms of withdrawal from the national public sphere. In addition, the rapid globalisation of arts and artistic production simply ensures that modern democratic regimes in the country cannot stop the bleeding of artistic labour outside the national sphere.

It is true that Brazilian human demography is very diverse and often regionally disconnected, with ethnic groups observing different customs, religious beliefs and lifestyles. Rio's own ambivalent status (as a regional social and financial articulation, and a post-colonial phantasmagoria far away from Nothern American and European cultural industries) is reflected in the ways its artistic sentiments promote policies of 'reaching out' to national peripheries and marginal discourses so as to fuse and traffic them abroad as new 'World Cultures' (on which consult Nagib, 2011). The process of 'reaching out' to repositories of ethnic memory is recognised as a global manifestation of post-colonial artistic movements with a mission to transmute earlier proletarian and folkloric modes of socialist realism into forms of what became part of magical realism in Latin America. The handover's cultural mosaic is not immediately available to global audiences and Rio's artistic directors and performers have to find effective ways to communicate its complexity. As a result, they have to speak in playful riddles on behalf of one of their country's most

DOI: 10.1057/9781137336323

desired cityscapes. Rio's handover spectacle rested on the aestheticised consumption of Brazilian exoticism, keeping at bay colonial phantoms just enough to capitalise on slave mobility's 'absent presence' (Herzfeld, 2002; Chaney, 1996; Sheller, 2003). De Sousa Santos (2000 in Barreira, 2011, p. 154; de Sousa Santos, 1999) speaks in this cultural context of a 'sociology of absences', the ability of institutional frameworks to erase or amplify disenfranchised voices that escape through cracks of officialdom into global spheres. The terms 'absent presence' and 'sociology of absences' do not point to the discourse of slavery per se, but revert instead to traces that Borgesian travellers redeem as tourist tokens (Thompson, 2012, p. 42). This is Rio's *articulation* writ large, complete with music, dance and joy, used by artistic apparatuses to invoke global (e)motions. Let us forget then London as an Olympic articulation and move our 'tourist' model to the other side of the Atlantic.

4.2   Brazilian beauty: situating the beholder's eye

The section's introduction with the Greek national anthem and the London Mayor, Boris Johnson's passing of the Olympic Flag to the Mayor of Rio de Janeiro, Eduardo Paes, was followed by the Brazilian national anthem. Thereafter, '*Embrace*', created by Cao Hamburger and Daniela Thomas, unfolded as an attempt of the city's Organising Committee (ROCOG) to provide a segment 'full of joy and passion'. The very title compresses the principles of heartfelt hospitality any tourist host purports to have and to which all Olympic hosts subscribe in the European economy of giving. But Brazilian 'joy' and 'passion' add physicality in a term that propagates a model of the 'tourist body' as both a physical and an imaginary site (Veijola and Jokinen, 1994; Veijola and Valtonen, 2007). Notably, press reports suggested that the directors avoided stereotypical self-presentations of Brazilian culture in the handover (Segun, 12 August 2012). Thomas' admission was that the spectacle's clichés 'don't misrepresent us, but we want to show other ways in which we mix. We are very far from Europe and North America. [...] We get this information and we reinvent.[...] This is our spirit, this is how we produce [pop] culture' (Gibson and Kingsley, 10 August 2012). It is worth remembering that hybridity is as much an artistic as it is a political tool (Nederveen Pieterse, 2006a). As much as this book avoids a monological political scene, the directors' discourse of hybridity supports a Heideggerian version of 'The

DOI: 10.1057/9781137336323

Truth' in elevating hybridity as mixing to a value. Hidden behind this abstraction is a well-established disjunction between multi-culturalism as an ideal, and multi-cultural political realities that are 'shoved under the carpet' (Parekh, 2000). The fact that the handover's performances were framed by a collection of representations of Northeastern genres also flags the old question of ownership: who is cast as mere wage labour or elite artist and who takes full credit for the product beyond loyalties (Born and Hesmondhalgh, 2000, p. 26)? The old debate on recognition is constitutive of such global mobilities.

Brazilian Truth encompasses visions of a nascent culture, always ready to mature into a beautiful product. This young entity is playful like a childish tourist, dexterous like a pre-conscious body and in need to be put into new digital frames that favour what Ong (1982) describes as 'second orality'. But where modern colonisers instilled in the country the machine of scripture from outside, post-modern natives installed a spectacle machine originating in the country's urban centres (see Patke, 2000 on urban phantasmagorias). The incompleteness of the Brazilian cultural project is nicely encapsulated in the ancient Greek term *ómor-fos* that denotes the beautiful being (the equivalent of Brazilian *belo*). As opposed to *õraíos*, the beautiful of time that comes to pass and to *kallós*, the aesthetically and morally ideal being that conforms to Kantian notions of beauty, *ómorfa* beings appealed to the Pythagorean principles of symmetry and the architectonics of image, so to speak (the Brazilian *lindo/a* as part of human *physis* or physical nature). With an emphasis on surfaces and form, Pythagorean discourse communicates with Lucretius' combination of body and emotion that inspired Spinoza's observation on power geometries and the physical effects of human affects (general debate in Adey, 2010, pp. 164–5). Brazilian ethno-cultural *dispositions* to *omorfiá* created a European philosophical medley that at least in the contemporary discourse on sports confuses nurtured skills with ethno-racial (black) capacity (Bale, 2004).

Emerging from the European colonial project, Brazilian national articulations had to conform to some cosmetic cosmopolitan rules that framed civilisational beauty in terms of what we know as 'style' or character (Born and Hesmondhalgh, 2000, p. 20–1). But as mentioned in Chapter 1, 'character' is an ideal type in the context of the London 2012 ceremonies. De Pina Cabral (2008, pp. 234–5) suggested that European colonisation produced a bifurcated narrative of identity as otherness, a heterological trope akin to that we encounter in the ill-defined domain

DOI: 10.1057/9781137336323

of the Caribbean (Sheller, 2003 and 2004). Although centuries after colonisation Brazilian modes of art are still engaging in Western-style counter-colonial games (see Dikötter, 2008 and Law, 2010 for aspects of the debate on the racialisation of the world), globalisation imperatives replace the memory of slavery with narratives of lifestyle consumption, cinematic and tourist mobilities. Foreign observers espoused and globally disseminated the demonic trope to validate representations of specific human types and later on to produce thanatotourist tropes (Dann and Seaton, 2001). Following Mbembe's (2003) analysis of 'necropolitics' as the power inherent to death as a state of non-existence, Tate (2011) suggests that this oscillation between terror, love and romance allows for the production of a critical post-colonial discourse in which choosing to die (as native sacrifice) responds to the Western *anthropophagies* of tourism, sex trafficking and racist idealisation. But this sacrificial revolt has not always been successful. In many ways, Kantianism landed on Brazilian soil the moment European settlers discovered this otherworldly, 'demonic' topos at once fearful and *ómorfos* in their writings. Such demonologies were accommodated into everyday life and turned into adventurous mind-walking rituals for global *flâneurs*.

The handover spectacle is such a paradoxical staging of Rio's *ómorfi* (*linda maravilhosa*) Brazil – a montage of cosmetic appearances that taunts spectators with commoditised absences in dance, music, modelling and other props. In the context of American cinema Denzin (2002) examines how the emergence of a 'new black aesthetic' codified a national crisis crowned by an intersectional vocabulary that coloured the otherness of class, gender and ethnicity in moral terms. Realist and idealist registers mingled to 'honour' and vilify black cultures. The handover to Rio presents us with such a cosmetic conflict in representations. The directors were chosen carefully to this end: screenwriter, TV and movie director Carlos Imperio or Cao Hamburger (b. 1962, São Paulo) became known for the *Castelo Rá-Tim-Bum* series of programs for children in TV, *Cultura of São Paulo*, which gave birth to a successful movie with the same title. He also directed in 2006 another successful film, *O Ano em Que Meus Pais Sairam de Férias* (The Year My Parents Went on Vacation), partly based on his childhood memories. His interest in children as cinematic subjects derives from his Rousseauian belief that they should be treated as intelligent human beings (IMDB, Cao Hamburger, undated). Rio-born (1959) Daniela Thomas is also a film and TV director and screenwriter (IMDB, Daniela Thomas: undated).

DOI: 10.1057/9781137336323

Both represent Brazil's urban artistic elite and are examples of affluent tourists- *tornadóroi*. As such, they were in a position to craft an intimate gaze of Brazilian pop culture and to enrich it with a complex of auditory and embodied narratives. Interestingly, their tourist grammar of joy hinged upon the Brazilian aesthetics of the vagabond, the black worker and the female dancer-model. By reinstating the cosmetic meaning of urban mobility, the directors brought Rio's Brazil closer to European and North American glamour industries. The ceremony confirmed that the city of Rio is, above all, a storeroom of tourist signs: its 'signature' bears the mark of trade, migration and culture – all things projecting marketable Brazilian uniqueness. As a collection of audio-visual signs Rio nicely accommodates the mechanic workings of the filmic and the tourist *tórnoi*. By sheer analogy to London's marketable Occidentalism, Rio revamped the practical Orientalist model (Herzfeld, 2006b) in line with global tourist imperatives. Above all, the artistic directors' propensity to *glocalise* artistic narratives of Brazilian culture(s) highlights interpenetrations of localities, regions and global spheres while also silencing tensions in the integrative project of Brazilian nation-building and Olympic community-building (on 'glocalisation' see Robertson, 1992).

4.3   Scene-by-scene

The segment commences when the stage is bathed in Brazil's national colours (green and yellow) and Renato Sorriso enters the arena in a street cleaner's uniform (complete with a broom) and begins to dance samba. Sorriso was a real street cleaner from the Rio Sambadrome who became cult hero when he was filmed dancing while he swept the streets. He is interrupted by sailor Robert Scheidt (São Paulo, 1973), who asks him to stop his performance but is eventually drawn into the rhythm. Scheidt is one of Brazil's most successful Olympian athletes with two gold medals, two silver medals and a bronze from five Olympic Games. Bringing together the civilised role of the sea and the plurality of 'low culture', the couple articulates Rio's mobile urban profile. Scheidt's clumsy emulation of Sorriso's dancing speaks a kinaesthetic language of civility: much like salsa and other Latin American genres, samba originates in street dancing that was organised into schools of working migrants in Brazil. Its association with historic slave mobilities from Africa and with Rio's favelas, which today serve as tourist sites, accentuates its twin meaning in the segment as thanatotourist rite and contemporary pop culture. The embodied and musical contribution of the segment recalls the function of the soundtracks in new national cinemas as vehicles for vernacular musics that begin to cross national borders: the famous bossa nova soundtrack for *Black Orpheus* in the late 1950s and the New World musics that took shape in the first half of the century – jazz, tango, samba, son. These styles 'became the basis and inspiration for an extraordinary profusion of local musical renaissances ranging from motown to bossa nova to juju to reggae' (Denning, 2001, pp. 362–3). The ineptitude of Sorriso's partner also reminds viewers that the mastery of samba dancing is a 'symbolic good' obtained though hard physical work without losing its aura as an exotic leisure activity (Crouch, 1999; Ritzer, 1999). Sorriso stands in the segment as an example of Brazil's embodied knowledge industry: not only is he literally a worker that achieved social recognition through his dancing skills, he is also a cinematic articulation of Sepucai, the annual meeting place for samba schools where he was originally discovered. Hamburger's and Thomas' introduction neatly corresponds to Danny Boyle's narrative of British industrialised modernity through selective remembrance of Brazil's folk-come-urban 'working body' (see also Hesmondhalgh's [2007, pp. 513–5] analysis of Frith's high/low aesthetics in music).

This symbolic tourist-national body becomes feminised in the ceremony, when a group of Brazilian samba dancers join Sorriso in the arena for a colourful sequence on Rio's spectacular economies. However, when Sorriso is also joined by popular Brazilian singer Marisa Monte, rapper BNegão, actor Seu Jorge and model Alessandra Ambrósio the segment begins to showcase Brazil's 'sign/culture industries' and the ways Rio as one of its infrastructural nodes becomes inserted into global articulations – of music, dance, cinema, fashion but also economies (Lash and Urry, 1994; Sassen, 2002). A few decades ago James Clifford (1988, p. 224) suggested that Western institutions construct taxonomies responsible for the production of authenticity that consign value to non-Western performances and ideas. Yet, such 'power-geometries of space-time compression' (Massey, 1993, p. 61) also enable flows and interconnections of human beings, ideas and cultural products that once stayed fixed and in isolation from world circuits. At the other end of the academic spectrum, Hesmondhalgh (1996, p. 201) has explained that the cultural politics of music can only be properly illuminated if we combine

DOI: 10.1057/9781137336323

an examination of the music's reception across cultures with the unequal distribution of power that this dissemination may conceal. Elsewhere he also discussed music through feminist critiques of elitism in support of ordinary aesthetic evaluation (Hesmondhalgh, 2007a, p. 509). Yet for others exotic dancing simply conceals the packaging of human beings as 'embodied commodities' behind an ennobling discourse of travel (Turner, 1994, pp. 21–2; Sánchez Taylor, 2000). There are connections to athletics to highlight here: Carrington's (2010) ethnographic study of notable British athletes explored the manner in which blackness, and indeed Englishness, has been contested through mass-mediated representations. At the same time, other scholars examined how non-white sport celebrities become representative embodiments of their community in popular media domains (Burdsey, 2007). Such outside-inside perspectives find an analogue in artistic genres and betray the omnipresence of *diforic* and *multiforic* trends in a globalised world. In fact, such trends reproduce the historical mobility of *tornadóros* from work to tourist economies of signs and space: for example, Western cinematic and musical tropes of blaxploitation that veered towards humorous and denigrating representations of race connect to even earlier narratives focusing on industry and labour practices – or what Wong (1978) terms 'role segregation' and 'role stratification' (Wiegman, 1998, pp. 160–4). Even though it is difficult to fix a normative response to Rio's global audio-visual and kinaesthetic flows, it is worth stressing that Jorge, Sorriso and the sambistas on the one hand, and Ambrósio on the other, articulate Brazil's polyvocalities in racial-as-cultural terms. The contrast between white (Ambrósio, Marisa Monte as an operatic singer who is dressed in white) and black (Sorriso, the samba dancers, the 'tribes' and most singers) reiterates Hollywood's enduring chiaroscuro technique as a sort of aestheticised boundary definition (Dyer, 1997). As a hybrid performance it does not entirely escape the Orientalist paradigm of opera genres that thrived on binary definitions and recurring structures of plot and character but promotes marginalities such as femininity and blackness to honourable core self-definitions (Born and Hesmondhalgh, 2000, p. 8 and pp. 50–1 [ftns pp. 24–9]).

We might promote this debate by stressing how, just like the symphonies of cinema, musical 'texts' both reflect and debate structures of tourism, especially because their lyrics become a site of contested meanings and changing community ideals (Mitchell, 1996; Malbon, 1999; Duffy, 2000; Tzanelli, [2007b] 2010, p. 131). This cosmological vortex dilutes in

DOI: 10.1057/9781137336323

global artscapes. However, its power to survive lies in the synaesthetic nature of cultural industries that trade sound with bodily performance, image and text. The introduction of Monte as Yemanja, a sort of goddess (orisha) of the religion called Candomblé, is part of the segment's thanatotourist mobilities: Candomblé is a kind of mesh of African religions and beliefs slaves brought to Brazil when it was still a colony. 'As a Water Queen, Yemanja is believed to steal sailors to be her lovers by drowning them in sea storms' (see Hernandez Foio, 12 August 2012). As an artist, Monte is an example of artscapes: whilst classically trained in opera singing, she grew up surrounded by the sounds of the Portela samba school, and combined diverse influences into her music. A world-traveller herself in the 1980s (she went to Italy where she met the famous producer Nelson Motta), she transformed herself into a hybrid of MPB diva and pop rock performer without repudiating traditional samba and folk musical origins (Wikipedia, 'Marisa Monte', undated). As Yemanja, Monte sang Bachiana No. 5 from the Bachianas Brasileiras, a group of nine suites by the Brazilian composer Heitor Villa-Lobos that was written for various combinations of instruments and voices between 1930 and 1945. Bachianas Brasileiras are examples of European and New World musical hybridities, fusions of Northeastern, native folk-popular music with Johann Sebastian Bach, and an attempt to adapt a number of Baroque harmonic and contrapuntal procedures to Brazilian music (Béhague, 1994). Bachiana No. 5 befits Brazilian cosmological darkness, as its lyrics speak of early evening's 'beauty and dreaming', the sadness of the Moon and a girl's desire to be pure and close to nature (Sattler, 15 July 2010). Within post-colonial Brazil the Northeast region was regarded as the bedspring of cultural authenticity early on, and became incorporated in statist attempts to attract global music-based tourism. The schizophrenic tendencies this produced originally within the nation (e.g. Northern ethno-racial diversity as a source of symbolic pollution) were resolved through Brazilian self-presentations in terms of a progressive cultural hybridity rather than degeneracy. This gave rise to the ideal of *branqueamento*, 'the belief that miscegenation would gradually and inexorably "whiten" and therefore "upgrade" the Brazilian population' (Skidmore, 1990). Monte later sang, alongside Brazilian performers BNegão and Seu Jorge, the bossa nova song 'Aquele Abraço' ('We Say Hello'), thus closing Rio's handover presentation with a different music style. Monte is in many respects the Brazilian equivalent of Western popera ('pop opera') movement, a blend of 'low order' craft with 'high

DOI: 10.1057/9781137336323

European' art on which *Brasilidade* (Brazilianness) is based as rooted self-narration yet a 'travelling culture'.

A Brazilian musician, singer, songwriter and actor, Seu Jorge was raised in a favela north of Rio de Janeiro which became known as the city of Belford Roxo (today part of Rio's larger metropolitan area). Jorge is considered by many as an artist that renewed Brazilian pop samba. He presents as major influences in his work various samba schools, but also American soul singer Stevie Wonder. In *City of God* (2002) Jorge played a good-looking 'ladies' man' who becomes a lost soul when a sociopath gangster kills everyone he loves out of spite. Seu Jorge adopted the role of the 'handsome, melancholy drifter with a mysterious past' in *The Life Aquatic with Steve Zissou* (2004) where he played the member of an oceanography crew who improvises Portuguese David Bowie covers (Garsd, 21 July 2010). Not only has this persona introduced American audiences to Jorge's music, it also made accessible to global audiences a fictitious – but reified – 'Brazilian character' shrouded in musical sadness. Jorge's propensity to sing of travellers' 'homecoming' journey (e.g. in 'Saudosa Bahia' from the 2010 album *Seu Jorge and Almaz* a traveller longs for beloved Bahia) likens the athletic *ánthropos'* Odyssean journey to an Olympic utopia. Hence, we might consider Jorge as a neo-pilgrim but also a facilitator of global neo-pilgrimages through music. Bringing together global discourses of poverty, social exclusion and migrant artscapes, Jorge's mobility from Rio's favela peripheries to the artistic centres of the West is symmetrical to Boyle's cinematic character (Jamal Malik) in *Slumdog Millionaire* who catapults from Indian slums to global fame thanks to his quiz skills.

Bernardo Santos, better known as BNegão (Rio de Janeiro, 1973), is a singer and songwriter of Brazilian rap and hip hop. Unlike Jorge's rooted favela profile, he launched his musical career through study, forming the band 'Perfeição Nenhuma Small Band e Engenharia de Som Ltda' ('Perfection No Small Band and Sound Engineering Ltd) that blended punk and electronic influences. Like Western rap, his songs are rife with socio-political criticism befit of the samba movement and its favelas context. BNegão became widely known for his album *Wiping the Ice* (2003), freely downloadable online via the band's website. This made him one of the first Brazilian artists to embrace the concept of Copyleft and Creative Commons (BNegão, 16 June 2004). His rough style which echoes the realist sentiment of Brazilian cinema stands in stark contrast to Ambrósio's cosmetic cosmopolitan style. Currently one of the

DOI: 10.1057/9781137336323

Victoria's Secret Angels, Ambrósio (born in Erechim, Rio Grande do Sul, 1981) has modelled for brands such as Next, Armani Exchange, Christian Dior, and Ralph Lauren. However, her profession represents another dimension of embodied and sexualised mobility that matches Brazilian pop culture's movement to Western consumerist terrains.

It is therefore significant that following Monte's singing as Yemanja, the stage is flooded with groups of performers in colourful costumes representing Brazil's exotic cultural mosaic and then BNegão's and Ambrósio's entrance. Dancing in exotic rhythms, the female sambistas in lighted costumes allow a party to commence that all performers join. In this sequence BNegão sang 'Maracatú Atomico' by Chico Science accompanied by samba school percussion (Jordan, 13 August 2012). Formerly known as Chico Science & Nação Zumbi, Chico Science is a Brazilian rock band that was formed by the now late Chico Science (1966–97). The musicians of the group continued as Nação Zumbi after his death in a car accident on 2 February 1997. Part of the Mangue Beat movement, their songs mix various styles including rock, punk, funk, hip hop, soul and Brazilian traditional music, with heavy use of percussion instruments (BBC Music, Nação Zumbi, undated). 'Maracatú Atomico' was written in memory of both interpreter Chico Science and composer Nelson Jacobina (1954–2012) as an articulation of maracatú, a Northeastern traditional Brazilian rhythm. Literally then a thanatotourist intervention in the spectacle, the song uses a marketable dialogics of recovery. Maracatú itself is a big chapter in contemporary formations of *Brasilidade*: the style's Northeastern 'origins' were mobilised by administrations in promotions of tourist-orientated carnival festivities and its alleged distinctiveness was fused in the discourse of samba as the nation's cultural capital (see also Sharp, undated).

The song's video clip showed to audiences with a knowledge of Rio's landscape what can be recognised as the narrow roads of Olinda that are crossed by maracatú musicians and fans. However, in the handover we are left with the song's lyrics in the place of these cityscape images. The song's festive character does precisely what Brazilian music is renowned for: it disguises sadness in upbeat rhythms for which other styles originating in African slavery are renowned. The lyrics carry this sadness in fusions of antithetical formalist motifs (nature and technology, obscuring and illumination). In a discourse bordering in places on surrealism, they speak of the ways the beak of a hummingbird kisses the 'hummingbird flower', making 'all fauna-flora cry of love'. Then in a clearer revolutionary

DOI: 10.1057/9781137336323

tone, the singer explains that art belongs to those holding 'the standard-bearer': such artists are the electron atomic maracatú band whose name the singer writes on black clouds 'just to show my attachment' (Meseta, 1 June 2012).

Ambrósio's grandstanding in the arrangement as a dancer seconded by Sorriso and other male participants is a manifestation of the new 'poetics of womanhood' (Herzfeld, 1985 on the 'poetics of manhood') that fashion feminine self-presentation on bodily aesthetics outside the public sphere, in clubs and (pop) domains of fandom. As the folk and the pop become audio-visually interlocked on stage, a new sequence introduces, through more samba music, a group carrying large pieces that unite in a representation of the famous street patterns in the Copacabana sidewalk. Samba, carnival costumes and symbols of the ludic beach replace the image of vagabond marginality with a tourist vision of Rio's city-node.

As an import from Portugal, the Carnaval is part of Brasilian legacies of authoritative defiance. A ceremony in its own right, carnivals promoted fusions of musical procession and *entrudos* or violent and aggressive pranks authorities soon would outlaw (Lee, 2012, p. 253). Combined international (European, Asian) and internal (people of

FIGURE 4.1 *The Rio 2016 procession, complete with Brazilian hybrid music, samba dancing and the Carnaval*

Source: Andrew Osborne/Flickr

DOI: 10.1057/9781137336323

African or mixed African and European ancestry from the Northeastern region) people moved to industrialised Rio de Janeiro in search of employment and formed on its hillsides the notorious favelas. Within these proto-industrial enclaves African and other diasporic traditions of Candomblé, capoeira (=ritual fights) and samba became identity markers but also banners of Afro-Brazilian protest before their translation into economic possibility in the global tourist trade (Shaw, 1999, p. 50). Especially samba's translatability into cultural and economic capital triggered battles over property rights 'in an informal popular culture that thrives on collaboration – but which is governed nonetheless by laws and contracts that have the power to determine one's wellbeing or position in society' (Davis, 2009, p. 13). This movement from Afro-Brazilian heritage to urban tourist legacy underscores the Olympic handover's hybrid pop-artistic dance sequences. It is not coincidental that the shift from informal to formal tourist economies was institutionalised during Getúlio Vargas' dictatorship (1930–45) with the calendrical formalisation of those art styles (Carnaval's designation to the 'impure' days before Ash Wednesday) and also the regulation of their content (each performance had to include an *enredo* or plot based on Brazilian history). Reflecting post-1940s European institutions of *scholé* as holidays for the working classes (see Dann and Parrinello 2009), these traumatic changes partook in later Brazilian articulations of 'human' as a being in (e)motion. Where working classness, abject ethnicity, unlawfulness and sin were placed by the Vargas administration in a continuum to validate the prevalence of the Catholic moral order, Rio's Olympic artwork placed dexterity, blackness, ritual bodily dialogue and hybrid music in the one emancipatory ludic category. Paying tribute to the first major Brazilian cinematic and musical projection of the favelas as an Edenic topos (*Orfeu Negro*, 1958) soon to open up to Europeans through long-distance holiday flights (Stam, 1989, pp. 176–7), the handover ceremony confirmed *Brasilidade's* global marketability.

Drawing upon Bourdieu's and Wacquant's (1992, p. 247) observations I contend that, just as any work of art might emerge from the belief system of the field of art (its 'magic') to partake in a domination system (centralised articulation), protest artwork communicates a constellation of meanings very specific to the transgressive cause (Löfgren, 1989; Hannerz, 1996; Hannerz and Löfgren, 1994; Titley, 2003, p. 5; Tzanelli, 2011). But such counter-articulations are infinitely more malleable than centralised legacies, so samba's and capoeira's integration into tourist mobilities and

DOI: 10.1057/9781137336323

their global dissemination by Olympic caravans as 'mind-walking' or audio-visual journey is unsurprising. In fact, both Sorriso and Scheidt's introductory sequence (of ritual dance) and the glowing 'tribes'' colourful dancing in the following sequence draw on the memoryscapes of the samba and capoeira complex through aggressive choreography, bodily signs (ethnic costumes, the performers' phenotypical 'blackness') and hybrid ethnic music. Browning (1995, p. 15), who contextualises samba rhythm as a negative form of articulation, a syncopated or silenced beat that choreographically narrates racial contact and conflict in the same space and time, examines in her study the un-European uniqueness of the genre. And just as pop samba, the embodied ritual dialogue of capoeira reiterates the European economy of (negative) reciprocities as an epistemology of silences or 'absent presence' (Herzfeld, 2002; Gordon, 2008; Lee, 2012; Tzanelli, 2011; Argyrou, 2013, forthcoming). The staged projection of the capoeira-samba encounter of a street cleaner with a well-dressed Olympic athlete encodes informal conflicts and socio-cultural registers.

Another Northeastern Brazilian phenomenon, capoeira is a 'game or sport in which [...] two contestants spar or dance to the rhythm of an ensemble of Afro-Brazilian instruments' (Lewis, 2000, p. 543). Its roots in the demonic domains of slave labour, masculine self-presentation and the black working body made it difficult for outsiders to acknowledge it as the equivalent of European duelling rituals. However, just as samba's organisation in schools, capoeira fighting was instituted in schools and in more recent years promoted to a type of tourist *scholé* through cultural industries. The handover's relevant sequence is nothing other than a manifestation of this mobility of the embodied *tórnos* (the working-class body struggling to attain certifiable duelling skills) to a televisual *tórnos* (the mechanical projection of this ritual as tourist pleasure). What had began as a 'streaming off' ritual in Northeastern regions of Brazil plagued by poverty and subjected to authoritarian state violence, would later migrate to Carnaval stages as a sort of ritualised venting (see Da Matta's, [1991] 'pressure valve' theory and De Certeau's, [1984] 'strategy' in social interaction) and even later to domains of cinematic-tourist fandom. The segment's transition from 'poperatic' to pop tunes is a continuation of this gendered tale of (e)motion that is not merely an outsider's stereotype, as Afro-Brazilian mock performances of capoeira in Bahia blend with tales of virility and sexual conquest. Monte, who first sang the Bachian suite, re-appears on stage to sing alongside BNegão and Seu Jorge the

DOI: 10.1057/9781137336323

bossa nova song 'Aquele Abraço' ('We Say Hello'). A lyrical fusion of samba and jazz, bossa nova became popular in the 1960s initially among young musicians and college students and later global jazz aficionados and professionals (Castro, 2003, p. 226). The popularisation of the trend coincided with the enlargement of global public spheres through political protest and socio-cultural movements (Veloso, 2003, p. 205).

In the next section the camera records a man disguised as Rio's traditional *Malandro do Morro*, literally the 'boy-man of bad mores', behind the entrance. Reflecting Western cinematic registers (Caine as Charlie Croacker), the *Malandro* is the lovable rogue that maintains a lifestyle of idleness, fast living and petty crime. Originating in Brazilian literature, cinema and music, samba lyrics celebrate this Bakhtinian 'character' as a folk hero defying authority and taking justice into his own hands (Shaw and Dennison, 2004). *Malandragem* was immortalised in a TV cigarette commercial in which former Brazilian soccer player Gérson de Oliveira Nunes utters 'I like to get an advantage in everything', and as a character trait, it retains some connotations to civility tropes. A comparative note on the diffusive origins of this literary-cinematic character might lead us back to Mannheim's (2003) musings on socio-artistic volition and to the very interactive nature of tourism. It seems that the mischievous boy-man – notably, a reflection of Dann's tourist as a spoilt and undisciplined child and Campbell's (2008, p. 28) analysis of ancient comedy as symbolic escape from *thanatos* – is widespread across Latin American cultures. For example, debating Cuban *jineteros* (literally horseback riders, by extension con men taking tourists 'for a ride'), Simoni (2008) propels scholars to consider some deployments of power in ambiguous encounters between tourists and Cubans as well as the implications these have for the function of tourism industries and the Cuban authorities. Various scholars highlighted the complexity of *jineterismo* that ties morality to national, racial and gendered discourses but also to romantic travel (Fernandez, 1999; Berg, 2004). Just as *malandragem*, *jineterismo* partakes in global circuits of rumours that simultaneously valorise and disempower subaltern ethnic types through emphasis on native tactical displays of affect, intimacy and sexuality in encounters with tourists looking for romance. The 'naturally hot' *caliente mulatta* and the 'naturally crafty' *jinetero/a* have evolved into globally mobile national traits (Sánchez Taylor, 2000; Tzanelli, 2007b; Fernandez, 2010). In sum, such representations confirm how exchanges of people and labour for money 'and the idolatry of things thus purchased emerges as a point where core

DOI: 10.1057/9781137336323

African-American values diverge from European ones' (Garner, 2007, p. 14). Fixed traits such as skin colour are however complemented with mobile ones, because these characters are understood and marketed in tourism via music genres such as salsa. Argentinian tango dancers, Brazilian *Malandros sambistas* and Cuban *salseros jineteros* are artistically understood as human types conforming to the principles of *vrotós*: seductive, alluring and athletic – mobile in more ways than one. Just as its equivalent in the Greek *mángas* or the tourist *kamáki*, the *Malandro* carries out an equalising social ritual where lack of status and class produce real inequalities (Shaw and Dennison, 2004, p. 22). The interchange of law and anti-law is a typical *leitmotif* in the Hollywood genre of confidence crime (Tzanelli et al. 2005) but its sexualisation in tourist encounters is even more persistent. In tourist contexts the *Malandro* is both actor – tricking (usually female) tourists – and acted upon – the object of the visitor's gaze (Cohen, 1986; Bowman, 1996, p. 3; Tsartas and Galani, 2009, p. 305; Tzanelli, 2011, pp. 133–5).

The *Malandro* also figures in capoeira's migration to the Carnaval that, especially in exotic Bahia, is habitually marked by violent and sexual acts involving machismo and other conventions considered of 'lower order' (Parker, 1991, p. 153; Lewis, 2000, pp. 547–9). Replacing the twin discourse of invisibility of colour (akin to assimilationism) and good exceptionalism with an 'embodied musical vocabulary' (Denzin, 2002, pp. 6, 8 and 21) transforms the *Malandro* into a contested commodity. Much like Brazilian cinema's twenty-first century turn to realist art, which involves bodily exposure, the *Malandro* operates on the normative level as a sort of (post) national exposure (see also Nagib, 2011, chapter 4). The Olympic projection of these tropes emphasises a hidden gender a-symmetry we also find in carnival play where men usually cross-dress (like the segment's colourful cast of male performers) but women undress (like the segment's samba dancers), go topless and often up on platforms (like Ambrósio) (Scherper-Hughes, 1992, p. 492 in Lewis 2000, p. 551). The economy of desire that frames the *Malandro* provides the Olympic spectator with a morsel of Brazilian cultural intimacy that is as embarrassing as it is endearing. Just as the *capoeira* and samba paradigms, his propensity to violence, mischief and trickery both promotes and challenges the hegemony of those standing outside his counter-culture as consumers and critics (Wacquant, 2001). As the guised trickster of the handover ceremony arrives at the centre of the Brazilian parade, Sorriso falls on his knees in a gesture of respect and then proceeds to embrace

DOI: 10.1057/9781137336323

him. We are aware that the segment is soon to come to a conclusion, so the embrace must be autopoetic ('Embrace' is the title of the segment). Articulations of Brazilian (e)motion are nicely encapsulated in the revelation that the stadium's trickster is Brazilian football legend Pelé or Edison Arantes do Nascimento (Três Corações, 1940). As the former footballer takes off his jacket, his number 10 T-shirt is revealed and fireworks erupt in the stadium. Representing the inner regions of Brazil (Northwest of Rio), Pelé is regarded by many as the best player of all times. His case is paradigmatic of the ways embodied craft socially compensates marginal personae, which in Brazil would otherwise be second-class citizens, with a cultural citizenship on the world stage. Pelé and Sorriso are the embodied analogues of Brazilian musical performance and they answer to what Middleton (2000) saw in post-Renaissance European strategy of assimilation and projection as ways of confronting difference. In 1999, Pelé was voted Football Player of the Century by the International Federation of Football History and Statistics in 1999 (IFFHS, undated). His identity as a Baumanesque world tourist ensured recognition within Brazil as a national hero. This compensation mechanism also includes his self-presentation as an ardent advocate of policies geared towards the improvement of social conditions for the poor, especially children (Encyclopaedia Britannica, 'Pelé', undated). In 1997 Pelé received an honorary Knight Commander of the Order of the British Empire from Queen Elizabeth II (*The Independent*, 4 December 1997), so his presence in the 2012 ceremony had an additional cosmopolitan meaning. Social standing aside, Pelé is known in print-capitalist circuits through his best-selling autobiographies, his starring in several successful documentary and semi-documentary films, and his composition of numerous musical pieces, including the soundtrack (Sergio Mendes) for the documentary *Pelé* (1977). In 2009 he cooperated with Ubisoft on arcade football game *Academy of Champions: Soccer* for the Wii in which he voiced-over the coach (Scullion, 2 June 2009). His sign value in global industrial systems makes him both a national and a transnational good – a new cosmopolitan subject.

It has been noted that international Premier Leagues have resorted to the integration of the 'highly stylized visual aesthetic and potent celebrity cachet of [...] cinema culture' into 'match-day entertainment and team branding' strategies (Rowe and Gilmour, 2009, p. 179). In contemporary sport the slow mobilities of the Olympic legend are framed by the fast of digital TV and cinema – especially where issues of ethno-racial

DOI: 10.1057/9781137336323

marginality are involved. Celebrity aura can be both a stereotyping and a liberating tool in this respect (see Carrington's [2010] work). Pelé's universally praised technique and natural athleticism are signs of Brazilian mobility, so his professional turn to global cultural industries is anything but unexpected (also MacAloon, 1997 on gender). It is worth noting that as he passes outside the national domain into cultural industrial systems, Pelé's value is also detached from conceptions of the human body and replaced by cyborg articulations of Brazilian dexterity. Pelé's persona in Rio 2016's segment fuses his speedy professional ethos with Brazil's slow cosmologies of trickery – an amicable marriage in the context of the Olympic event. During his time as UNESCO Goodwill Ambassador, Pelé proposed legislation to reduce corruption in Brazilian football, which became known as the 'Pelé law', but largely unfounded accusations that he was involved in corruption scandals put an end to this intervention (Reuters, 23 November 2001).

In his 'alterglobalising' ethic (Harvey et al., 2009) Pelé drifts disparate narratives (cinematic, digital, embodied) of (hu)man nature into a Brazilian variation of (pure, aspirational) *ánthropos* and (impure, lowly) *vrotós*. His post-retirement entrepreneurial trajectory in creative and athletic industries sustains the ambiguity of such meta-categories while also allowing playful articulations of Brazil's unique cultural timeline through the black, male, working but touring body. Although Christian Neoplatonic understandings of Pelé-the-human take a back seat in the Olympic industry, their cultural translatability across the world is a useful audio-visual tool. Pelé is, of course, exemplary of the discourse of *scholé* in that he was consciously implicated in various educational, cinematic and tourist projects. He therefore remains a carrier of the Cartesian duality that haunts Olympic industries and their travel circuits (Touraine, 1995). The technopoetic role of such personae in cyborg-like projections of host cities as global financial articulations (see Kellogg et al., 1991; Mitchell, 2003) might also explain his ceremonial positioning as a marketable 'crafty' character. As fluid as Rio's seafaring self-narration in the concluding segment on London 2012, Pelé-the- *tornadóros* revisits the Brazilian trauma *par excellence*: the 'Discovery of the Exotic Human' that will set in motion the project of multiple modernities.

DOI: 10.1057/9781137336323

Bibliography

Abramovitch, S. (14 August 2012) 'George Michael responds to critics of his Olympics performance', Hollywood Reporter, http://www.hollywoodreporter.com/earshot/george-michael-responds-critics-whitelight-olympics-361871, date accessed 16 September 2012.

Academy of Achievement (undated) 'Julie Andrews', http://www.achievement.org/autodoc/page/andobio-1, date accessed 9 September 2012.

Adey, P. (2010) *Mobility* (London: Routledge).

Adler, J. (1992) 'Mobility and the creation of the subject: Theorizing movement and the Self in early Christian monasticism', *International Tourism- Between Tradition and Modernity Colloquium* (Nice, France), 407–15.

Albrow, M. (1997) 'Travelling beyond local cultures: Socioscapes in a global city', in J. Eade (ed.) *Living the Global City* (London: Routledge), 7–55.

Albrow, M., J. Eade, J. Dürrschmidt and N. Washbourne (1997) 'The impact of globalization on sociological concepts: Community, culture and milieu', in J. Eade (ed.) *Living the Global City* (London: Routledge), 20–36.

Anderson, B. (1991) *Imagined Communities* (London: Verso).

Appadurai, A. (1981) 'The Past as a scarce resource', *Man*, 16(2), 201–19.

Appadurai, A. (1990) 'Disjuncture and difference in the global cultural economy', *Public Culture*, 2(2), 1–24.

ArchelorMittal Orbit (undated) http://www.london.gov.uk/sites/default/files/Mittal%20brochure.pdf, date accessed 4 September 2010.

DOI: 10.1057/9781137336323

Archer, M. (1995) *Realist Social Theory* (Cambridge: Cambridge University Press).

Archer, M. (1996) *Culture and Agency*, rev. edn. (Cambridge: Cambridge University Press).

Arendt, H. (1958) *The Human Condition* (Chicago: University of Chicago Press).

Argyrou, V. (2005) *The Logic of Environmentalism* (Oxford: Berghahn).

Argyrou, V. (2013 [forthcoming]) *The Gift of European Thought and the Cost of Living* (Oxford: Berghahn).

Aristotle (1946) *Politics* (Oxford: Clarendon).

Aristotle (1996) *Poetics* (London: Penguin).

Attwood, F. (2002) 'Reading porn: The paradigm shift in pornography research', *Sexualities*, 5(1), 91–105.

Bailey, N. and N. Winchester (2012) 'Islands in the stream: Methodological nationalism under conditions of globalization', *Sociology*, 46(4), 712–27.

Bærenholdt, O., M. Haldrup, J. Larsen, and J. Urry (2004) *Performing Tourist Places* (Aldershot: Ashgate).

Bajc, V., S. Coleman and J. Eade (2007) 'Mobility and centering in pilgrimage', *Mobilities*, 2, 321–9.

Bakhtin M.M. (1968) *Rabelais and His World*, translated by H. Isowolsky (Cambridge, MA: MIT).

Bakhtin M.M. (1981) *The Dialogic Imagination*, edited by M. Holquist (Austin, TX: Texas University Press).

Bakhtin, M.M. (1984) *Problems of Dostoevsky's Poetics* (Manchester: Manchester University Press).

Bakhtin, M.M. (1986) *Speech Genres and Other Essays* (Austin: University of Texas Press).

Bal, M. (2003) 'Visual essentialism and the object of visual culture', *Journal of Visual Culture*, 2(1), 5–32.

Bale, J. (2004) *Running Cultures* (London: Routledge).

Barney, R. K. (2006) 'A simple souvenir: The Wienecke Commemoration medal and Olympic victory celebration', *Olympika*, 15, 87–112.

Barreira, I.A.F. (2011) 'Social movements, culture and politics in the work of Brazilian sociologists', *Latin American Perspectives*, 38(3), 150–68.

Barthes R. (1993) *Mythologies* (London: Vintage).

Bataille, G. (1988) *The Accursed Share* (New York: Zone Books).

DOI: 10.1057/9781137336323

Bateson, G. (1980) *Mind and Nature* (London: Fontana).

Baudrillard, J. (1983) *Simulations* (New York: Semiotext).

Baudrillard, J. (1988) *Selected Writings*, edited by M. Poster (Stanford, CA: Stanford University Press).

Bauman, Z. (1976) *Socialism* (London: Hutchinson).

Bauman, Z. (1987) *Legislators and Interpreters* (Ithaca, N.Y.: Cornell University Press).

Bauman, Z. (1991) *Modernity and Ambivalence* (Cambridge: Polity).

Bauman, Z. (1992) *Intimations of Postmodernity* (London: Routledge).

Bauman, Z. (1998) *Globalization* (New York: Columbia University Press).

Bauman, Z. (2000) *Liquid Modernity* (Cambridge: Polity).

Bauman, Z. (2005) *Liquid Life* (Cambridge: Polity).

Bauman, Z. (2007) *Liquid Times* (Cambridge: Polity).

BBC Entertainment and Arts (13 August 2012) 'Profile: Kim Gavin, director of Olympic closing ceremony', http://www.bbc.co.uk/news/entertainment-arts-19094398, date accessed 13 September 2012.

BBC Music (undated) 'Nação Zumbi – Biography', http://www.bbc.co.uk/music/artists/e3954b21-0d05-45ea-a057-e8cc4c9b1ab5, date accessed 24 September 2012.

BBC Sport (12 August 2012) 'BBC records Imagine for Olympics finale', http://www.bbc.co.uk/sport/0/olympics/19235606, date accessed 20 September 2012.

BBC Sport (12 August 2012) 'Olympic ceremonies: Closing ceremony in 3D', http://www.bbc.co.uk/programmes/b01m315q, date accessed 12 September 2012.

Beck, M. (28 August 1970) 'Julie Andrews tries charity work', *Milwaukee Journal*, http://news.google.com/newspapers?nid=1499&dat=1970082 8&id=lNojAAAAIBAJ&sjid=UCgEAAAAIBAJ&pg=7113,4107216, date accessed 9 September 2012.

Beck, U. (1992) *Risk Society* (London: Sage).

Beck, U. (1999) *World Risk Society* (Cambridge: Polity).

Beck, U. (2000) 'The cosmopolitan perspective: Sociology of the second age of modernity', *British Journal of Sociology*, 51, 79–105.

Beck, U. (2005) *Power in the Global Age* (Cambridge: Polity).

Beck, U. and E. Beck-Gernshein (1995) *The Normal Chaos of Love* (Cambridge: Polity).

Beck, U., A. Giddens, and S. Lash (1994) *Reflexive Modernization* (Cambridge: Polity).

Becker, H.S. (1982) *Art Worlds* (Berkeley: University of California Press).

DOI: 10.1057/9781137336323

Becker, H.S., R.R. Faulkner and B. Kirshenblatt-Gimblett (2006) 'Introduction' in H.S. Becker, R.R. Faulkner and B. Kirshenblatt-Gimblett (eds) *Art from Start to Finish* (Chicago: University of Chicago Press), 1–21.

Bederman G. (1995) *Manliness and Civilization* (Chicago: University of Chicago Press).

Béhague, G. (1994) *Heitor Villa-Lobos: The Search for Brazil's Musical Soul* (Austin: Institute of Latin American Studies, University of Texas at Austin).

Bell, M.M. and M. Gardiner (1998) 'Bakhtin and the human sciences: A brief introduction', in M.M. Bell and M. Gardiner (eds) *Bakhtin and the Human Sciences* (London: Sage), 1–12.

Benhabib, S. (1992) *Situating the Self* (New York: Routledge).

Benjamin, T. (2009) *The Atlantic World* (Cambridge: Cambridge University Press).

Benjamin, W. (1973) *Understanding Brecht*, translated by A. Bostok (London: Verso).

Benjamin, W. (1989) 'The work of art in the age of mechanical reproduction', in D. Richter (ed.) *The Critical Tradition* (New York: St. Martin's Press).

Benjamin, W. (1992[1968]) *Illuminations* (London: Fontana Press).

Bennett, A. (1995) *The Birth of the Museum* (London: Routledge).

Benson, A.M. (2011) *Volunteer Tourism* (New York: Routledge).

Berg, M.L. (2004) 'Tourism and the revolutionary New Man: The specter of jineterismo in late "Special Period" Cuba', *Focaal*, 43, 46–56.

Bergson, H. (1950) *Matter and Memory* (London and New York: Allen and Unwin).

Berking, H. (1999) *Sociology of Giving* (London and New Delhi: Sage/Theory, Culture and Society).

Berners-Lee, T. (undated) 'Frequently asked questions, start of the web: Influences', World Wide Web Consortium, http://www.w3.org/People/Berners-Lee/FAQ.html#Influences, date accessed 7 October 2012.

Bernstein, A. (2000) ' "Things you can see from there you can't see from here": Globalization, media and the Olympics', *Journal of Sport and Social Issues*, 24(4), 351–69.

Bhabha H.K. (1994) *The Location of Culture* (London and New York: Routledge)

DOI: 10.1057/9781137336323

Bhatt, C. (2000) 'Primordial being: Enlightenment, Schopenhauer and the Indian subject of postcolonial theory', *Radical Philosophy*, 100, 28–41.

Billig, M. (1995) *Banal Nationalism* (London: Sage).

Billings, A. (2008) *Olympic Media* (London: Routledge).

Billintgon, M. (13 August 2013) 'London 2012 closing ceremony', *The Guardian*, http://www.guardian.co.uk/sport/2012/aug/13/london-2012-olympic-games-closing-ceremony-review?INTCMP=SRCH, date accessed 13 September 2013.

Billington, M. (13 August 2012) 'London 2012 closing ceremony – review', *The Guardian* http://www.guardian.co.uk/sport/2012/aug/13/london-2012-olympic-games-closing-ceremony-review, date accessed 20 March 2013.

Bilton, R. (11 August 2012) 'Olympics: Closing ceremony "party" details promised', BBC News UK, http://www.bbc.co.uk/news/uk-19211950, date accessed 12 September 2012.

Binkley, S. (2000) 'Kitsch as a repetitive system: A problem for the theory of taste hierarchy', *Journal of Material Culture*, 5(2), 131–52.

BNegão (16 June 2004) 'BNegão in copyleft', CMI Brasil, http://www.midiaindependente.org/pt/red/2004/06/283492.shtml, date accessed 22 September 2012.

Bio.truestory (2012) 'J.K. Rowling', http://www.biography.com/people/jk-rowling-40998, date accessed 20 March 2012.

Bolan, P. and N. O'Connor (2008) 'Creating a sustainable brand for Northern Ireland through film induced tourism', *Tourism, Culture & Communication*, 8(3), 147–58.

Borges, J.L. (1998) *Collected Fictions* (New York: Viking).

Born, G. and D. Hesmondhalgh (2000) *Western Music and its Others* (Chicago: University of California Press).

Bott, E. (2004) 'Working on a working class utopia: Marking young Britons in Tenerife on the new map of European migration', *Journal for Contemporary European Studies*, 12(1), 57–70.

Bourdieu, P. (1977) *Outline of a Theory of Practice*, translated by R. Nice (Cambridge: Polity Press).

Bourdieu, P. (1997) 'Selections from the logic of practice', in A. D. Schrift (ed.) *The Logic of the Gift* (London: Routledge), 190–230.

Bourdieu, P. (1998) *Practical Reason* (Cambridge: Polity).

Bourdieu, P. and R. Nice (1980) 'The aristocracy of culture', *Media, Culture & Society* 2(3), 225–54.

DOI: 10.1057/9781137336323

Bourdieu P. and L.J.D. Wacquant (eds) (1992) *An Invitation to Reflexive Sociology* (Chicago: University of Chicago Press).

Bowles M.J. (2003) 'The practice of meaning in Nietzsche and Wittgenstein', *Journal of Nietzsche Studies*, 26(1), 14–24.

Bowman, G. (1996) 'Passion, power and politics in a Palestinian tourist market', in T. Selwyn (ed.) *The Tourist Image* (New York: John Wiley & Sons), 83–103.

Boyd, D. and N. Ellison (2007) 'Social network sites: Definition, history and scholarship', *Journal of Computer-mediated Communication*, 13(1), http://jcmc.indiana.edu/vol13/issue1/boyd.ellison.html, date accessed 13 May 2012.

Brecht, B. (1964 [1936]) *Brecht on Theatre* (London: Shevan Press).

Brennan, T. (2003) *The Transmission of Affect* (Ithaca, NY: Cornell University Press).

Browning, B. (1995) *Samba* (Bloomington, IN: Indiana University Press).

Burdsey, D. (2007) *British Asians and Football* (London: Routledge).

Buroway, M. (1979) *Manufacturing Consent* (Chicago: University of Chicago Press).

Buschman, J. and K. L. Lennartz, (1996) 'From Los Angeles (1932) to Melbourne (1956): The Olympic Torch's protagonism in ceremonies', in M. De Moragas, J. MacAloon and M. Llines (eds) *Olympic Ceremonies* (Lausanne: International Olympic Committee), 111–30.

Butler, J. (1993) *Bodies that Matter* (London: Routledge).

Campbell, C. (2005) *The Romantic Ethic and the Spirit of Modern Consumerism* (Oxford: Blackwell/Alcuin Academics).

Campbell, J. (2008) *The Hero with a Thousand Faces* (California: New World).

Campbell, J.K. (1964) *Honour, Family and Patronage* (Oxford: Oxford University Press).

Carrington, B. (2010) *Race, Sport and Politics* (London: Sage).

Carruthers, M. (1998) *The Craft of Thought* (Cambridge: Cambridge University Press).

Cashman, R. and B. Harris (2012) *The Australian Olympic Caravan from 2000 to 2012* (Petersham, NSW: Walla Walla Press).

Castells, M. (1996) *The Rise of the Network Society* (Oxford: Blackwell).

Castoriadis C. (1987) *The Imaginary Institution of Society*, translated by K. Blamey (Cambridge, MA: Harvard University Press).

Castro, R. (2003) *Bossa Nova* (Chicago: Cappella Books).

DOI: 10.1057/9781137336323

Cavanagh, A. (2007) *Sociology in the Age of the Internet* (Buckingham: OUP).

Cavanaugh, W. (2008) 'Migrant, tourist, pilgrim, monk: Mobility and identity in a global age', *Theological Studies*, 69, 340–56.

Caves, R.E. (2002) *Creative Industries* (Cambridge, MA: Harvard University Press).

Cere, R. (2002) 'Digital counter-cultures and the nature of electronic social and political movements', in Y. Jewkes (ed.) *Dot.cons: Crime, Deviance and Identity on the Internet* (Tavinstock, Devon: Willan), 147–63.

Chalip, L., B.C.Green, , and L. Vander Velden. (2000) 'The effects of polysemic structures on Olympic viewing', *International Journal of Sports Marketing and Sponsorship*, 2(1), 39–57.

Chaney, D. (1996) *Lifestyles* (London: Routledge).

Chatterjee P. (1986) *Nationalist Thought and the Colonial World* (Minneapolis, MN: University of Minnesota Press).

Chatterjee P. (1993) *The Nation and its Fragments* (Princeton, NJ: Princeton University Press).

China.org.cn (undated) 'Behind the 29th Olympic Opening Ceremony', http://www.china.org.cn/olympics/news/2008–08/10/content_16182023.htm, date accessed 13 September 2012.

Chouliaraki, L. (2008) 'The media as moral education: Mediation as action', *Media, Culture & Society*, 30(6), 831–52.

Chowdry, G. (2007) 'Edward Said and contrapuntal reading: Implications for critical interventions in international relations', *Millennium*, 36(1), 101–16.

Christaller, W. (1955) 'Contributions to a geography of tourism', *Erdkunde*, 9, 1–19.

Clark K. and M. Holquist (1984) *Mikhail Bakhtin* (Cambridge, MA: Harvard University Press).

Clifford, J. (1988) *The Predicament of Culture* (Cambridge, MA: Harvard University Press).

Clifford, J. (1992) 'Travelling cultures', in L. Grossberg, C. Nelson and P. Treichler (eds) *Cultural Studies* (New York: Routledge), 96–116.

Clifford, J. (1997) *Routes* (Cambridge, MA: Harvard University Press).

Cloke, P. and H. C. Perkins (1998) ' "Cracking the canyon with the awesome foursome": Representations of adventure tourism in New Zealand', *Environment and Planning D: Society and Space*, 16(2), 185–218.

DOI: 10.1057/9781137336323

Cohen, A.P. (1992) 'Self-conscious anthropology', in J. Okely and H. Callaway (eds) *Anthropology and Autobiography* (London: Routledge), 221–41.

Cohen, E. (1986) 'Lovelorn farangs: The correspondence between foreign men and Thai girls', *Anthropological Quarterly*, 59(3), 115–27.

Cohen, E. (1996) 'The sociology of tourism: approaches, issues and findings', in Y. Apostolopoulos, S. Leivadi and A. Yannakis (eds) *The Sociology of Tourism* (London: Routledge), 51–71.

Cohen, S.A. (2011) 'Lifestyle travellers: Backpacking as a way of life', *Annals of Tourism Research*, 38(4), 117–33.

Connell, R.W. (1987) *Gender and Power* (Stanford, CA: Stanford University Press).

Connell, R.W. (1995) *Masculinities* (Berkeley, CA: University of California Press).

Connerton, P. (1989) *How Societies Remember* (Cambridge: Cambridge University Press).

Conversi, D. (2001) 'Cosmopolitanism and nationalism', in A. Leoussi and A.D. Smith (eds) *The Companion Guide to Nationalism* (New Brunswick: Transaction), 34–9.

Couldry, N. (2003a) 'Media meta-capital: Extending the range of Bourdieu's field theory', *Theory and Society*, 32(5/6), 653–77.

Couldry, N. (2003b) *Media Rituals* (New York: Routledge).

Couldry, N. (2006) *Listening Beyond the Echoes* (Boulder, CO: Paradigm).

Coyne, R. (1999) *Technoromanticism* (Boston, MA: MIT).

Cresswell, T. (2010) 'Towards a politics of mobility', *Environment and Planning D; Society and Space*, 28(1), 17–31.

Crossley, N. (2003) 'From reproduction to transformation: Social movement fields and the radical habitus', *Theory, Culture & Society*, 20(6), 43–68.

Crouch, D. (1999) 'Encounters in leisure/tourism', in D. Crouch (ed.) *Leisure/Tourism Geographies* (London: Routledge), 1–16.

Crouch, D and L. Desforges (2003) 'The sensuous in the tourist encounter: The power of the body in tourist studies', *Tourist Studies*, 3(1), 5–22.

Cunningham, S. (2005) 'Creative enterprises', in J. Hartley (ed.) *Creative Industries* (Oxford: Blackwell), 282–98.

Currah, A. (2007) 'Managing creativity: The tensions between commodities and gifts in a digital networked environment', *Economy and Society*, 36(3), 467–94.

DOI: 10.1057/9781137336323

Da Matta, R. (1991) *Carnivals, Rogues and Heroes* (Notre Dame, IN: University of Notre Dame Press).

Dallmayr, F. (2001) *Beyond Orientalism* (New Delhi: Rawat).

Dann, G.M.S. (1977) 'Anomie, ego-enhancement and tourism', *Annals of Tourism Research*, 4, 184–94.

Dann, G.M.S. (1988) 'Tourism, peace and classical disputation', in L. D'Amore and J. Jafari (eds) *Tourism* (Montreal: Colour Art), 25–33.

Dann, G.M.S. (1989) 'The tourist as a child: Some reflections', *Cahiers du Tourisme Série C*, 135.

Dann, G.M.S. (1996) *The Language of Tourism* (Wallingford: CABI).

Dann, G.M.S. (1998) 'There's no business like old business: Tourism, the nostalgia industry of the future', in W.F. Theobald (ed.) *Global Tourism*, 2nd edn. (Oxford: Butterworth Heinemann), 29–43.

Dann, G.M.S. and E. Cohen (1996) 'Sociology and tourism', in Y. Apostolopoulos, S. Leivadi and A. Yannakis (eds) *The Sociology of Tourism* (London: Routledge), 301–14.

Dann, G.M.S. and G. Liebman Parrinello (2009) 'Setting the scene', in G.M.S. Dann and G. Parrinello (eds) *The Sociology of Tourism* (UK: Emerald), 1–63.

Dann, G.M.S. and A. V. Seaton (2001) 'Slavery, contested heritage and thanatourism', in G.M.S. Dann and A.V. Seaton (eds) *Slavery, Contested Heritage and Thanatourism* (New York: Haworth Hospitality Press), 1–29.

Davis, D.J. (2009) *White Face, Black Mask* (Michigan: Michigan State University Press).

Davis, J. (1987) 'Family and state in the Mediterranean', in D. Gilmore (ed.) *Honor and Shame and the Unity of the Mediterranean* (Washington: American Anthropological Association), 22–34.

Davis, M. (2008) *Freedom and Consumerism* (Aldershot: Ashgate).

de Certeau, M. (1984) *The Practice of Everyday Life* (Berkeley, CA: University of California Press).

de Certeau, M. (1986) *Heterologies* (Manchester: Manchester University Press).

de la Fuente, E. (2007) 'The "new sociology of art": Putting art back into social science', *Cultural Sociology*, 1(3): 409–25.

De Moragas, M., N. Rivenburgh. and J.F. Larson. (2002) 'Opening ceremony narratives', in W.L. Adams, and L.R. Gerlach (eds) *The Olympic Games, Ancient and Modern* (Boston, MA: Pearson Custom Publishing), 191–206.

DOI: 10.1057/9781137336323

De Pina-Cabral, J. (2008) 'Sarakatsani reflections on the Brazilian Devil', in M. Mazower (ed.) *Networks of Power in Greece* (London: Hurst), 233–56.

De Sousa Santos, B. (1995) *Towards a New Common Sense* (New York: Routledge).

De Sousa Santos, B. (1999) 'Towards a multicultural conception of human rights', in M. Featherstone and S. Lash (eds) *Spaces of Culture* (London: Sage), 214–29.

Deacon A. (2007) 'Civic labour or doulia? Care, reciprocity and welfare', *Social Policy and Society*, 6(4), 481–90.

Debord, G. (1995) *Society and the Spectacle* (New York: Zone).

Degun, T. (12 August 2012) 'Pelé surprises London 2012 Closing Ceremony crowd with Rio 2016 handover performance', Inside the Games, http://www.insidethegames.biz/olympics/summer-olympics/2012/18228-pele-surprises-london-2012-closing-ceremony-crowd-with-rio-2016-handover-performance-, date accessed 21 September 2012.

Delanty, G. (2000) *Modernity and Postmodernity* (London: Sage).

Delanty, G. (2006) 'The cosmopolitan imagination: Critical cosmopolitanism and social theory', *The British Journal of Sociology*, 57(1), 25–47.

Delanty, G. and P. O'Mahony (2002) *Nationalism and Social Theory* (London: Sage).

Deleuze, G. and F. Guattari (1988) *A Thousand Plateaus* (London: Athlone).

Denning, M. (2001) 'Globalization in cultural studies: Process and epoch', *European Journal of Cultural Studies*, 4(3), 351–64.

Dennis, K. and J. Urry (2009) *After the Car* (Cambridge: Polity).

DeNora, T. (2000) *Music and Everyday Life* (Cambridge: Cambridge University Press).

DeNora, T. (2003) *After Adorno* (Cambridge: Cambridge University Press).

Denzin, N. (2002) *Reading Race* (London: Sage).

Dora, Della V. (2007) 'Putting the world into a box: A geography of nineteenth-century "travelling landscapes"', *Geografiska Annaler*, 89B, 287–306.

Derrida, J. (1994) *Spectres of Marx* (New York: Routledge).

Derrida, J. and A. Dufourmantelle (2000) *Of Hospitality* (Stanford, CA: Stanford University Press).

DOI: 10.1057/9781137336323

Desforges, L. (2000) 'Traveling the world: Identity and travel biography', *Annals of Tourism Research*, 27(4), 926–45.

Devlin, E. (19 August 2012) 'London 2012 Olympics: Why we reinvented the Union flag for the Closing Ceremony', *The Telegraph*, http://www. telegraph.co.uk/sport/olympics/london-2012/9484348/London-2012-Olympics-why-we-reinvented-the-Union-flag-for-the-Closing-Ceremony.html, date accessed 13 September 2012).

Dickmann, A. and K. Hannam (2012) 'Touristic mobilities in India's slum places', *Annals of Tourism Research*, 39(3), 1315–36.

Dikötter, F. (2008) 'The racialization of the globe: An interactive interpretation', *Ethnic and Racial Studies*, 31(8), 1478–96.

DiMaggio, P. (1982) 'Cultural entrepreneurship in 19th century Boston', *Culture and Society*, 4, 440–55.

Douglas, M. (1992) *Risk and Blame* (London: Routledge).

Douglas, M. (1993) *Purity and Danger* (London: Routledge).

Douglas, M. and A. Wildaski (1982) *Risk and Culture* (Berkeley, CA: University of California Press).

Dubin, S. (1987) *Bureaucratising the Muse* (Chicago: University of Chicago Press).

Duffy, M. (2000) 'Lines of drift: Festival participation and performing a sense of place', *Popular Music*, 19(1), 51–64.

Dürrschmidt, J (1997) 'The delinking of locale and milieu', in J. Eade (ed.) *Living the Global City* (London: Routledge), 56–72.

Duval, D.T. (2007) *Tourism and Transport* (Wallingford: CABI).

Dyer, R. (1997) *White* (London: Routledge).

Dyson, E. (1998) Release 2.1: A Design for Living in a Digital Age (London: Penguin).

Eade, J. (1992) 'Pilgrimage and tourism at Lourdes, France', *Annals of Tourism Research*, 19(1), 18–32.

Eade, J. (2001) *Placing London* (Oxford: Berghahn).

Eagleton, T. (2000) *The Idea of Culture* (Oxford: Blackwell).

Earl, B. (2008) 'Literary tourism: Constructions of value, celebrity and distinction', *International Journal of Cultural Studies*, 11(4), 401–17.

Edensor, T. (2001) 'Performing tourism, staging tourism: (Re)producing tourist space and practice', *Tourist Studies*, 1(1), 59–81.

Edensor, T. (2004) 'Automobility and national identity: Representation, geography and driving practice', *Theory, Culture & Society*, 21(4), 101–20.

DOI: 10.1057/9781137336323

Edensor, T. (2005) 'Mediating William Wallace: Audio-visual technologies in tourism', in D. Crouch, R. Jackson and F. Thompson (eds) *The Media and the Tourist Imagination* (New York: Routledge), 105–18.

Elias N. (1996) *The Germans*, translated by E. Dunning and S. Mennell (New York: Columbia University Press).

Elias N. (2006) *The Court Society*, translated by E. Jephcott (Dublin: University College Dublin Press).

Encyclopaedia Britannica (undated) 'Pelé', http://www.britannica.com/EBchecked/topic/449124/Pele, date accessed 22 September 2012.

Engel, M. (2008) 'Variants of the Romantic *Bildungsroman*', in G. Gillespie, M. Engel and B. Dieterle (eds) *Romantic Prose Fiction* (Amsterdam: John Benjamins), 263–95.

Fabian, J. (1983) *Time and the Other* (New York: Columbia University Press).

Fabian, J. (1999) 'Theatre and anthropology, theatricality and culture', *Research in African Literatures*, 30(4), 24–31.

Faulkner, K. (13 August 2012) 'Twitter backlash at appearance of Kate Moss and Naomi Campbell after Olympics Stadium was turned into a giant catwalk', *The Daily Mail*, http://www.dailymail.co.uk/news/article-2187447/London-2012-closing-ceremony-Twitter-backlash-appearance-Kate-Moss-Naomi-Campbell.html#ixzz26duKyjpF, date accessed 16 September 2012.

Faulkner, K. (13 August 2012) ' "Gold medal for phone throwing": Twitter backlash at appearance of Kate Moss and Naomi Campbell after Olympics Stadium was turned into a giant catwalk', The Daily Mail, http://www.dailymail.co.uk/news/article-2187447/London-2012-closing-ceremony-Twitter-backlash-appearance-Kate-Moss-Naomi-Campbell.html, date accessed 20 March 2013.

Featherstone, M. (1991) 'The body in consumer culture', in M. Featherstone (ed.) *The Body* (London: Sage), 1–35.

Fernandez, N. (1999) 'Back to the future? Women, race, and tourism in Cuba', in K. Kempadoo (ed.) *Sun, Sex, and Gold* (Lanham: Rowman & Littlefield), 81–97.

Fernandez, N. (2010) *Revolutionizing Romance* (New Brunswick, NJ: Rutgers University Press).

Fish, R. (2003) 'Mobile viewers: Media producers and the televisual tourist', in D. Crouch, R. Jackson and F. Thompson (eds), *The Media and the Tourist Imagination* (New York: Routledge), 119–34.

DOI: 10.1057/9781137336323

Fischer, M. (2004) 'Integrating anthropological approaches to the study of culture: The "hard" and the "soft"', *Cybernetics and Systems*, 35(2/3), 147–62.

Fischer, M., D. Lyon and D. Zeitlyn (2008) 'The Internet and the future of social science research', in *The Sage Handbook of Online Research Methods* (London: Sage), 519–36.

Fortes, M. (1969) *Kinship and the Social Order* (Chicago, IL: Aldine de Guyter).

Foucault, M. (1979) *The History of Sexuality*, I, translated by R. Hurley (London: Allen Lane).

Foucault, M. (1986) 'Of other spaces', *Diacritics*, 16(1), 22–7.

Foucault, M. (1994) *The History of Sexuality*, II (Harmondsworth: Penguin).

Foucault, M. (1997) 'The birth of biopolitics', in P. Rabinow (ed.) *Michel Foucault* (New York: New Press), 73–9.

Foucault, M. (2003) Abnormal: Lectures at the College de France, 1974–5 (New York: Picador).

Fraser D.P. and W.J. Brown (2002) 'Media, celebrities, and social influence: Identification with Elvis Priestley', *Mass Communication and Society*, 5(2), 183–206.

Freud, S. (1948) *Totem and Taboo* (New York and Toronto: Vintage).

Freud, S. (1967) *Moses and Monotheism* (New York: Random House).

Freud, S. (1982) Sigmund Freud: Introductory Lectures of Psychoanalysis (London: Penguin).

Freud, S. (2002) *Civilization and its Discontents* (London: Penguin).

Freudendal-Pedersen, M. (2009) *Mobility in Daily Life* (Aldershot: Ashgate).

Friedberg, A. (1993) *Window Shopping* (Berkeley, CA: University of California Press).

Friedberg, A. (1995) 'Cinema and the postmodern condition', in L. Williams (ed.) *Viewing Positions* (Brunswick, NJ: Rutgers University Press), 59–86.

Frow, J. (1998) 'Is Elvis a God? Cult, culture, questions of method', *International Journal of Cultural Studies*, 1(2), 197–210.

Fullagar, S. (2012) 'Gendered cultures of slow travel', in S. Fullagar, K. Markwell and E. Wilson (eds) *Slow Tourism* (Bristol: Channel View), 99–112.

Fuller, P. (1988) *Seeing through Berger* (London: Claridge Press).

Funkenstein, A. (1986) *Theology and the Scientific Imagination* (Princeton: Princeton University Press).

DOI: 10.1057/9781137336323

Fussell, P. (1975) *The Great War and Modern Memory* (New York: Oxford University Press).

Gabriel, B. (2004) 'The unbearable strangeness of Being', in B. Gabriel and S. Ilcan (eds) *Postmodernism and the Ethical Subject* (Montreal: McGill-Queen's University Press), 149–202.

Gallant T.W. (2002) *Experiencing Dominion* (Notre Dame, IN: University of Notre Dame Press).

Garner, S. (2007) *Whiteness* (London: Taylor and Francis).

Garrison, J.W. (1996) 'Practical notes: Brazilian NGOs from grassroots to national civic leadership', *Development and Practice*, 6, 250–4.

Garsd, J. (21 July 2010) 'First listen: Seu Jorge, "Seu Jorge and Almaz"', NPR Music, http://www.npr.org/2010/07/21/128647674/first-listen-seu-jorge-seu-jorge-and-almaz, date accessed 22 September 2012.

Geertz, C. (1973) *The Interpretation of Cultures* (New York: Basic Books).

Geertz, C. (1980) *Negara* (Princeton, NJ: Princeton University Press).

Geertz, C. (1986) *Works and Lives* (Cambridge: Polity Press).

Germann Molz, J. (2004) 'Playing online and between the lines: Round-the-world websites as virtual places to play', in M. Sheller and J. Urry (eds) *Tourism Mobilities* (London: Routledge), 167–80.

Garnham, N. (1990) *Capitalism and Communication* (London: Sage).

Garnham, N. (2000) *Emancipation, Media and Modernity* (Oxford: Oxford University Press).

Gavin, K. Personal Website (undated) 'Biography', http://kimgavin.com/biog.html, date accessed 13 September 2012.

Gibson, O. and P. Kingsley (10 August 2012) 'Olympic closing ceremony to bring samba to Stratford', *The Guardian*, www.guardian.co.uk/sport/2012/aug/10/olympic-games-2012-closing-ceremony, date accessed 9 September 2012.

Gibbons, J. (2007) *Contemporary Art and Memory* (London: I.B.Tauris).

Giddens, A. (1984) *The Constitution of Society* (Berkeley: University of California Press).

Giddens, A. (1985) *The Nation-State and Violence* (Cambridge: Polity).

Giddens, A. (1987) *Social Theory and Modern Sociology* (Cambridge: Polity).

Giddens, A. (1990) *The Consequences of Modernity* (Cambridge: Polity).

Giddens, A. (1991) *Modernity and Self-Identity* (Cambridge: Polity).

Giddens, A. (2002) *Runaway World* (London: Routledge).

Gilroy, P. (1993) *The Black Atlantic* (London: Verso).

DOI: 10.1057/9781137336323

Glancey, J. (1 April 2010) 'First among Olympian odelisks', *The Guardian*, http://www.guardian.co.uk/uk/2010/apr/01/london-kapoor, date accessed 4 September 2012.

Gledhill, C. (1987) 'The melodramatic field: An investigation', in C. Gledhill (ed.) *Home is Where Heart Is* (London: BFI), 5–39.

Giulianotti, R. and R. Robertson (2004) 'The globalization of football: A study in the glocalization of the "serious life"', *The British Journal of Sociology*, 55(4), 545–68.

Gouldner, A.W. (1960) 'The norm of reciprocity: A preliminary statement', *American Sociological Review*, 25, 161–78.

Gouldner, A.W. (1973) 'The importance of something for nothing', in R.C. Hinkle Jr and G.J. Hinkle (eds) *For Sociology* (New York: Basic Books), 260–90.

Gourgouris, S. (1996) *Dream Nation* (Stanford, CA: Stanford University Press).

Gourlay, C. and C. Ruiz (25 October 2009) 'Look out, Paris, Boris plans a "Piffle Tower"', *The Sunday Times*.

Gordon, A. (2008) *Ghostly Matters* (Minneapolis: University of Minnesota Press).

Graburn, N.N.H. (1983) *To Pray, Pay and Play* (Aix en-Provence: Centre des Hautes Etudes Touristiques).

Graburn, N.H.H. (2001) 'Relocating the tourist', *International Sociology*, 16(2), 147–58.

Graml, R. (2004) '(Re)mapping the nation: Sound of Music tourism and national identity in Austria, ca 2000', *Tourist Studies*, 4(2), 137–59.

The Guardian Poll (31 March 2010) 'Olympic heights', http://www.guardian.co.uk/commentisfree/poll/2010/mar/31/architecture-design, date accessed 4 September 2010.

Guttman, A. (2006) 'Berlin 1936: The most controversial Olympics', in A. Tomlinson and C. Young (eds) *National Identity and Global Sports Events* (New York: SUNY), 65–78.

Haas, P. (1992) 'Knowledge, power and international policy coordination', *International Organization*, 46(1), 1–35.

Habermas, J. (1989a) *The New Conservatism*, translated by S.E. Nicholsen (Cambridge, MA: MIT).

Habermas, J. (1989b) The Structural Transformation of the Public Sphere (Oxford: Polity).

Habermas, J. (1989c) *The Theory of Communicative Action*, II (Boston, MA: Beacon Press).

DOI: 10.1057/9781137336323

Habermas, J. (1996) *Between Facts and Norms*, translated by W.Rehg (Oxford: Polity).

Halbwachs, M. (1992) *On Collective Memory*, edited by L.A. Coser (Chicago: University of Chicago Press).

Haldrup, M. and J. Larsen (2003) 'The family gaze', *Tourist Studies*, 3: 23–46.

Haldrup, M. and J. Larsen (2010) *Tourism, Performance and the Everyday* (London: Routledge.)

Halgreen, T. (2004) 'Tourists in the concrete desert', in M. Sheller and J. Urry (eds.) *Tourism Mobilities* (London: Routledge), 143–54.

Hall, C., M. Dieter and K. Müller (2004) *Tourism, Mobility, and Second Homes* (Toronto: Channel View).

Hall. M. and A. Williams (2002) *Tourism and Migration* (Irvine: Springer).

Hall, S. (1992) 'The question of cultural identity', in S. Hall, D. Held and A. MacGrew (eds) *Modernity and its Futures* (Cambridge and Milton Keynes: Polity and Open University Press), 274–316.

Hall, S. (1996) 'When was the "post-colonial? Thinking at the limit', in I. Chambers and L. Curti (eds) *The Post-Colonial Question* (New York: Routledge), 242–60.

Hand, M. (2012) *Ubiquitous Photography* (Cambridge: Polity).

Hand, M. and B. Sandywell (2002) 'E-topia as Cosmopolis or Citadel', *Theory, Culture & Society*, 19(1/2), 197–225.

Hannam, K. and D. Knox (2010) *Understanding Tourism* (London: Sage).

Hannam, K., M. Sheller and J. Urry (2006) 'Editorial: Mobilities, immobilities and moorings', *Mobilities*, 1(1), 1–22.

Hannerz, U. (1990) 'Cosmopolitans and locals in world culture', *Theory, Culture & Society*, 7(2), 237–51.

Hannerz, U. (1996) *Transnational Connections* (London: Routledge).

Hannerz, U. and O. Löfgren (1994) 'The nation in the global village', *Cultural Studies*, 8, 198–207.

Hardt, M. and A. Negri (2000) *Empire* (Cambridge, MA: Harvard University Press).

Harré, R. (1986) *Varieties of Realism* (Oxford: Blackwell).

Harrington, A. (2004) *Art and Social Theory* (Cambridge: Polity).

Harvey, D. (1999) *The Limits to Capital* (London: Verso).

Harvey, J., J. Horne. and P. Safai (2009) 'Alterglobalization, global social movements, and the possibility of political transformation through sport', *Sociology of Sport Journal*, 26, 383–403.

DOI: 10.1057/9781137336323

Haybron, D. (2008) 'Philosophy and the science of subjective wellbeing', in M. Eid and R. Larsen (eds) *The Science of Subjective Well Being* (New York: Guildford), 17–43.

Hebdige, D. (1979) *Subculture* (London: Routledge).

Hennion, A. and B. Latour (1993) *La Passion Musicale* (Paris: Editions Métalié).

Hernandez Foio, N. (12 August 2012) 'A breakdown of Rio's Olympic presentation', http://lucidoutlooks.wordpress.com/2012/08/12/a-breakdown-of-rios-olympic-presentation/, date accessed 21 September 2012.

Herzfeld, M. (1980) 'Honour and shame: Problems in comparative analysis of moral systems', *Man*, 15(2), 339–51.

Herzfeld, M. (1985) *The Poetics of Manhood* (Princeton, NJ: Princeton University Press)

Herzfeld M. (1992) The Social Production of Indifference (Oxford: Berg).

Herzfeld, M. (1997) 'Anthropology and the politics of significance', *Social Analysis*, 4(3), 107–38.

Herzfeld, M. (2002) 'The absent presence: Discourses of crypto-colonialism', *South Atlantic Quarterly*, 101(4), 899–926.

Herzfeld, M. (2004) *The Body Impolitic* (Chicago: University of Chicago Press).

Herzfeld, M. (2005) *Cultural Intimacy*, 2nd edn. (New York and London: Routledge).

Herzfeld, M. (2006a) 'Spatial cleansing: Monumental vacuity and the idea of the West', *Journal of Material Culture*, 1(1/2), 127–14

Herzfeld, M. (2006b) 'Practical Mediterraneanism', in W.V. Harris (ed.) *Rethinking the Mediterranean* (Oxford: Oxford University Press), 45–64.

Herzfeld, M. (2007) 'Global kinship: Anthropology and the politics of knowing', *Anthropological Quarterly*, 80(2), 313–23.

Heidegger, M. (1967) *Being and Time* (Oxford: Blackwell).

Heywood, S. (2004) 'Informant disavowal and the interpretation of storytelling revival', *Folklore*, 115, 45–63.

Hibbert, C. (1969) *The Grand Tour* (London: Weidenfeld and Nicolson).

Hochschild, A. (1983) *The Managed Heart* (Berkeley: University of California Press).

Hodges, P. (24 April 2012) 'What does it really mean to be British?', *The Telegraph*, http://blogs.telegraph.co.uk/news/danhodges/100152734/

DOI: 10.1057/9781137336323

what-does-it-really-mean-to-be-english-nothing-at-all-and-thats-how-it-should-be/, date accessed 8 September 2012.

Hoesterey, I. (2001) *Pastiche* (Bloomington, IN: Indiana University Press).

Hogan, J. (2003) 'Staging the nation: Gendered and ethnicized discourses of national identity in Olympic Opening Ceremonies', *Journal of Sport and Social Issues*, 27, 100–23.

Holt, D.B., J. Quelch and E.L. Taylor (2004) 'How global brands compete', *Harvard Business Review* (Cambridge MA: University of Harvard Press), 68–75.

Honneth, A (1979) 'Communication and reconciliation: Habermas' critique of Adorno', *Telos*, 39, 45–69.

hooks, b. (1992) 'Eating the Other: Desire and resistance', in b. **hoo**ks (ed.) *Black Looks* (Boston: South End Press), 21–39.

Hutcheon, L (1988) *A Poetics of Postmodernism* (London and New York: Routledge).

Hutcheon, L. (1989) *The Politics of Postmodernism* (London and New York: Routledge).

Hutcheon, L. (2001) *A Theory of Parody* (Chicago, IL: University of Illinois Press).

Hesmondalgh, D. (1996) 'Popular music after rock and soul', in J. Curran, D. Morley and V. Walkerdine (eds) *Cultural Studies and Communications* (London: Arnold), 195–212.

Hesmondhalgh, D. (2007a) 'Aesthetics and everyday aesthetics: Talking about good and bad music', *European Journal of Cultural Studies*, 10(4), 507–27.

Hesmondhalgh, D. (2007b) *The Cultural Industries*, 2nd edn. (London: Sage).

Hesmondhalgh, D. and S. Baker (2010) *Creative Labour* (London: Routledge).

Honneth, A. (1979) 'Communication and reconciliation: Habermas' critique of Adorno', *Telos*, 39, 45–69.

Honneth, A. (1991) *The Critique of Power* (Cambridge, MA: MIT).

Honneth, A. (1992) *The Struggle for Recognition* (Cambridge: Polity).

Honneth, A. (2007) *Disrespect* (Cambridge: Polity).

Houlihan, B. and M. Green (2008) 'Comparative elite sport development', in B. Houlihan and M. Green (eds) *Comparative Elite Sport Development* (Oxford: Butterworth-Heinemann), 218–41.

DOI: 10.1057/9781137336323

Howard, C. (2012) 'Speeding up and slowing down: Pilgrimage and slow travel through time', in S. Fullagar, K. Markwell and E. Wilson (eds) *Slow Tourism* (Bristol: Channel View), 11–24.

Hutchinson J. (2004) 'Myth against myth: The nation as ethnic overlay', in M. Guibernaeu and J. Hutchinson (eds) *History and National Destiny* (Oxford: Blackwell), 109–24.

Hutnyk, J. (1996) *The Rumour of Calcutta* (London and New Jersey: Zed).

Huyssen, A. (1995) *Twilight Memories* (London: Routledge).

Huyssen, A. (2000) 'Present pasts: Media, politics, amnesia', *Public Culture*, 12(1), 21–38.

Hviid Jacobsen, M. (2012) 'Liquid modern "utopia"', in M. Hviid Jacobsen and K. Tester (eds) *Utopia* (Farnham: Ashgate), 69–96.

Hviid Jacobsen, M. and K. Tester (2012) 'Utopia as a topic for social theory', in M. Hviid Jacobsen and K. Tester (eds) *Utopia* (Farnham: Ashgate), 1–6.

IFFHS (undated) 'The world's best player of the century (World rankings)', http://www.iffhs.de/?42d03e32a16f43809fa3c17c13c09e20a1 5ff3c09f32b17f7370eff3702bb1c2bbb6e28fc380de43110f83d00e09, date accessed 22 September 2012.

Illouz, E. (2008) *Saving the Modern Soul* (Berkeley: University of California Press).

IMDB (undated) 'Cao Hamburger', http://www.imdb.com/name/ nm0357463/bio, date accessed 21 September 2012.

IMDB (undated) 'Charlie Croacker', http://www.imdb.com/character/ ch0006111/bio, date accessed 14 September 2012.

IMDB (undated) 'Daniela Thomas', http://www.imdb.com/name/ nm0858680/, date accessed 21 September 2012.

IMDB (undated) 'Stephen Daldry', http://www.imdb.com/name/ nm0197636/, date accessed 13 September 2012.

The Independent (4 December 1997) 'Education: Sir Péle lends his support', http://www.independent.co.uk/news/education-sir-pele-lends-his-support-1286703.html, date accessed 22 September 2012.

Inglis, D. (2005) 'The sociology of art: Between cynicism and reflexivity', in D. Inglis and J. Hughson (eds) *The Sociology of Art* (London: Palgrave), 98–109.

Inglis, D. and R. Robertson (2004) 'Beyond the gates of the Polis: Reconfiguring sociology's ancient inheritance', *Journal of Classical Sociology*, 4(2), 165–89.

Ingold, T. (2000) *The Perception of the Environment* (London: Routledge).

DOI: 10.1057/9781137336323

Ingold, T. (2010) 'Ways of mind-walking: reading, writing, painting',
  Visual Studies, 25(1), 15–23.

Jafari, J. (1987) 'Tourism models: The sociocultural aspects', *Tourism
  Management*, 8(2): 151–9.

Jameson, F. (1991) Postmodernism, or, the Cultural Logic of Late
  Capitalism (Durham: Duke University Press).

Jay, M. (1993) *Downcast Eyes* (Berkeley: University of California Press).

Jenks, C. (1993) *Culture* (London and New York: Routledge).

Jordan, L. (13 August 2012) 'Rio receives Olympic flag in London',
  The Rio Times, http://riotimesonline.com/brazil-news/rio-
  sports/2016olympics/rio-receives-olympic-flag-in-london/#, date
  accessed 24 September 2012.

Kandinsky, W. (1982) *Complete Writings on Art*, I (1901–21) and II
  (1922–43), edited by K. C. Lindsay and P. Vergo (London: Faber &
  Faber).

Kellner, D. (2003) *Media Spectacle* (London: Routledge).

Kellogg, W.A., J.M. Carroll, and J.T. Richards (1991) 'Making reality a
  cyberspace', in M. Benedikt (ed.) *Cyberspace* (Cambridge, MA: MIT),
  411–31.

Kirshenblatt-Gimblett, B. (1998) *Destination Culture* (Berkeley, CA:
  University of California Press).

Kittay E.F. (2001) 'A feminist public ethic of care meets the new
  communitarian family policy', *Ethics*, 111, 523–47.

Kohn, N. and L. Love (2001) 'This, that and the other: Fraught
  possibilities of the souvenir', *Text and Performance Quarterly*, 21(1),
  1–17.

Kopytoff, I. (1986) 'The cultural biography of things: Commodification
  as process', in A. Appadurai (ed.) *The Social Life of Things* (Cambridge:
  Cambridge University Press), 64–91.

Krippendorf, J. (1987) *The Holiday Makers* (Oxford: Heinemann).

Krishna, A. and J. Nederveen Pieterse (2009) 'Inequality, culture and
  globalization in emerging societies: Reflections on the Brazilian
  case', in J. Nederveen Pieterse and B. Rehbein (eds) *Globalization and
  Emerging Societies* (Basingstoke: Palgrave Macmillan),

Kristeva, J. (1991) *Strangers to Ourselves*, translated by L.S. Roudiez (New
  York: Columbia University Press).

Kyriakidou, M. (2008) 'Rethinking media events in the context of a
  global public sphere: Exploring the audience of global disasters in
  Greece', *Communications*, 33(3), 273–91.

DOI: 10.1057/9781137336323

Lacan, J. (1998) The Four Fundamental Concepts of Psychoanalysis (London: Vintage).

Lanfant, F.M. (2009) 'Roots of the sociology of tourism in France', in G.M.S. Dann and G. Liebmann Parinello (eds) *The Sociology of Tourism* (UK: Emerald), 95–130.

Langford, B. (2005) *Film Genre* (Edinburgh: Edinburgh University Press).

Larsen, J. (2005) 'Families seen photographing: The performativity of tourist photography', *Space and Culture*, 8(4), 416–34.

Larsen, J., J. Urry and K.W. Axhausen (2006) 'Networks and tourism: Mobile social life', *Annals of Tourism Research*, 34(1), 244–62.

Lash, S. and J. Urry (1987) *The End of Organised Capitalism* (Madison, WI: University of Wisconsin Press).

Lash, S. and J. Urry (1994). *Economies of Signs and Space* (London: Sage).

Lau, R.W.K. (2011) 'Tourist sights as semiotic signs: A critical commentary', *Annales of Tourism Research* 38(2), 711–14.

Law, I. (2010) *Racism and Ethnicity* (London: Pearson Education).

Leach, B. (14 January 2009) 'Slumdog Millionaire director Danny Boyle almost became a priest', *The Telegraph*, http://www.telegraph.co.uk/culture/film/4238043/Slumdog-Millionaire-director-Danny-Boyle-almost-became-a-priest.html, date accessed 19 August 2012.

Lee. P. (2012) 'Carnavals and cultural cannibals: The political economy of samba and carnaval', *The Global Studies Journal*, 4(1), 253–62.

Lenhardt, C. (1975) 'Anamnestic solidarity: The proletariat and its manes', *Telos*, 25, 133–54.

Lennon, J. and M. Foley (2000) *Dark Tourism* (London: Continuum).

Lévi-Strauss, C. (1964) *Totemism* (London: Merlin Press).

Lew, A. (2011) 'Tourism's role in the global economy', *Tourism Geographies*, 9(3), 148–51.

Lewis, L.J. (2000) 'Sex and violence in Brazil: Carnaval, capoeira and the problems of everyday life', *American Ethnologist*, 26(3), 539–57.

Lienhard, J.H. (1999) 'Poets in the Industrial Revolution', *The Engines of our Ingenuity*, 1413, http://www.uh.edu/engines/epi1413.htm, date accessed 8 September 2012.

Löfgren, O. (1989) 'The nationalisation of culture', *Ethnologica Europaea*, 19(1), 5–24.

London 2012 Olympic Games (2012) *Opening Ceremony* (London: The London Organising Committee of the Olympic Games and Paralympic Games).

DOI: 10.1057/9781137336323

Luhmann, N. (2000) *Art as a Social System* (Stanford, CA: Stanford University Press).

Luhrmann, T.M. (1994) *Persuasions of the Witch's Craft* (London: Picador).

Lury, C. (2004) *Brands* (London: Routledge)

MacAloon, J. (1978) 'Religious themes and structures in the Olympic movement and the Olympic games', in F. Landry and W. Orban (eds) *Philosophy, Theology and History of Sport* (Miami: Symposia Specialists).

MacAloon, J. (1997) *Brides of Victory* (Oxford: Berg).

MacAloon, J. (2003) 'Cultural legacy: The Olympic Games a "world cultural property"', in M. De Moragas, C. Kennett and N. Puig (eds) *The Legacy of the Olympic Games, 1984-2000* (Lausanne: International Olympic Committee), 271–8.

MacAloon, J. (2006) 'The theory of spectacle: Reviewing Olympic ethnography', in A. Tomlinson and C. Young (eds) *National Identity and Global Sports Events* (New York: SUNY), 15–39.

MacAloon, J. (2008) '"Legacy" as managerial/magical discourse in contemporary Olympic affairs', *International Journal of the History of Sport*, 25(14), 2060–71.

MacCannell, D. (1989) *The Tourist* (London: Macmillan).

MacCannell, D. (2012) 'On the ethical stake in tourism research', *Tourism Geographies*, 14(1), 183–94.

Mackenzie J. (1997) *Empires of Nature and the Nature of Empires* (East Linton: Tuckwell Press).

Mauss, M. (1954) *The Gift* (London: Cohen & West).

McClintock, A. (1995) *Imperial Leather* (New York: Routledge).

Maffesoli, M. (1996) *The Time of the Tribes* (London: Sage).

Maguire, J. A. (1999) *Global Sport* (Cambridge: Polity).

Maguire, J. and M. Falcous (eds) (2010) *Sport and Migration* (London and New York: Routledge).

Malbon, B. (1999) *Clubbing* (London: Routledge).

Mannheim, K. (1968 [1936]) *Ideology and Utopia* (New York: Harcourt, Brace & World).

Mannheim, K. (2003) 'The dynamics of spiritual realities', in J. Tanner (ed.) *The Sociology of Art* (London: Routledge), 215–20.

Maoz, D. (2006) 'The mutual gaze', *Annals of Tourism Research*, 33, 221–39.

Marcuse, H. (1955) *Eros and Civilization* (New York: Beacon Press).

DOI: 10.1057/9781137336323

Massey, D. (1993) 'Power-geometry and a progressive sense of place', in B. Curties, G. Robertson and L. Tickner (eds) *Mapping the Futures* (London and New York: Routledge), 59–69.

Massey, D. (1994) *Space, Place and Gender* (Cambridge: Polity).

Mauss, M. (1954) *The Gift* (London: Free Press).

Mbembe, A. (2003) 'Necropolitics', translated by L. Meintjes, *Public Culture*, 15(1), 11–40.

McKee, R. (1999) *Story* (London: Methuen).

McLuhan, M. (1962) *The Guttenberg Galaxy* (London: Routledge and Kegan Paul).

McLuhan, M. (1964) *Understanding the Media* (New York: McGraw).

McRobbie, A. (2002) 'Clubs to companies: Notes on the decline of political culture in speedup creative worlds', *Cultural Studies*, 16(4), 517–31.

Melucci, A. (1995) 'The process of collective identity', in H. Johnston and B. Klandermas (eds) *Social Movements and Culture* (Minneapolis: University of Minnesota Press), 41063.

Meseta (1 June 2012) 'Chico Science and Nação Zumbi, "Maracatú Atomico" by Jacobina/Mautner', *The Rumor Mill News Reading Room*, http://www.rumormillnews.com/cgi-bin/archive. cgi?noframes;read=241335, date accessed 24 September 2012.

MetroLyrics.com (undated) 'Read All About It (III). Emeli Sande', http://www.metrolyrics.com/read-all-about-it-part-iii-lyrics-emeli-sande.html#ixzz26WMJmNBi, date accessed 15 September 2012.

Middleton, R. (2000) 'Musical belongings: Western music and its low-other', in G. Born and D. Hesmondhalgh (eds) *Western Music and its Others* (Chicago: University of California Press), 59–85.

Misztal, B. (2003) *Theories of Social Remembering* (Maidenhead, Philadelphia: Open University Press).

Mitchell, T. (1996) *Popular Music and Local Identity* (London: Leicester University Press).

Mitchell, W. J. (2003) *ME++: The Cyborg Self and the Networked City* (Cambridge, MA: MIT).

Mitchell, W.J.T. (1994) *Landscape and Power* (Chicago: University of Chicago Press).

Malfas M., E. Theodoraki and B. Houlihan (2004) 'Impacts of the Olympic Games as mega-events', *Municipal Engineer* (Paper 13568), 157: 209–20.

DOI: 10.1057/9781137336323

Moir, J. (13 August 2013) Our musical heritage? Oh, pull the other one', *The Daily Mail*, http://www.dailymail.co.uk/news/article-2187509/Our-musical-heritage-Oh-pull-Jan-Moirs-Olympic-Closing-Ceremony.html#ixzz26LJBQv7L, date accessed 13 September 2013.

Molotch, H. (2004) 'How art works: Form and function in the stuff of life', in R. Friedland and J. Mohr (eds) *Matters of Culture* (Cambridge: Cambridge University Press), 341–77.

Moreiras, A. (1999) 'The order of order: On the reluctant culturalism of anti-subalternist critiques', *Journal of Latin American Cultural Studies*, 8(1), 125–45.

Moreiras, A. (2001) *The Exhaustion of Difference* (Durham: Duke University Press).

Mulvey, L. (2006) 'Visual pleasure and narrative cinema', in M.G. Durham and D.M. Kellner (eds) *Media and Cultural Studies* (Oxford: Blackwell), 342–52.

Murashov, I. (1997) 'Bakhtin's carnival and oral culture', in C. Adlam, R. Falconer, V. Makhlin and A. Renfrew (eds) *Face to Face* (Sheffield: Sheffield Academic Press), 203–13.

Nagib, L. (2011) *World Cinema and the Ethics of Realism* (New York: Continuum).

Nash, C. (2000) 'Performativity in practice: Some recent work in cultural geography', *Progress in Human Geography*, 24(4), 653–64.

Neale, S. (2000) *Genre and Hollywood* (London: Routledge).

Nederveen Pieterse, J. (2006a) 'Globalization as hybridization', in M.G. Durham and D. Kellner (eds) *Media and Cultural Studies* (Malden: Blackwell), 658–80.

Nederveen Pieterse, J. (2006b) 'Emancipatory cosmopolitanism: Towards an agenda', *Development and Change*, 37(6), 1247–57.

Nederveen Pieterse, J. (2009) 'Multipolarity means thinking plural: Modernities', *Protosociology*, 1(26), 19–35.

Nederveen Pieterse, J. (2011) 'Discourse analysis in international development studies', *Journal of Multicultural Discourses*, 6(3), 237–40.

Nederveen Pieterse, J. (2012) 'Many Renaissances, many modernities?', *Theory, Culture & Society*, 28(3), 149–60.

Nederveen Pieterse, J. and B. Parekh (eds) (1995) *The Decolonization of Imagination* (London: Zed).

Nervo Codato, A. (2006) 'A political history of the Brazilian transition from military dictatorship to democracy', translated by M. Adelman, *Revista Sociologia e Política*, 25(2), 83–106.

DOI: 10.1057/9781137336323

Neumann, M. (1988) 'Wandering through the museum: Experience and identity in a spectator culture', *Borderlines*, 12, 19–27.

Nietzsche, F.W. (1996) *On the Genealogy of Morals* (Oxford: Oxford University Press).

NNB (undated) 'David Bowie', http://www.nndb.com/people/076/000023007/, date accessed 18 September 2012.

Nora, P. (1989) 'Between memory and history: Les lieux de emoire', *Representations*, 26(2), 7–25.

O'Brien, M. (2008) *A Crisis of Waste?* (New York: Routledge).

Official London 2012 Website (2012) http://www.london2012.com/, date accessed 1 September 2012.

Ong, W. (1982) *Orality and Literacy* (London: Routledge).

Palmer, C. (1999) 'Tourism and the symbols of identity', *Tourism Management*, 20, 313–21.

Pattullo, P. (1996) *Last Resorts* (London: Cassell-Latin American Bureau).

Parekh, B. (2000) *Rethinking Multiculturalism* (London: Macmillan).

Parker, R. (1991) *Bodies, Pleasures and Passions* (Boston: Beacon Press).

Parkins, W. (2004) 'Out of time: Fast subjects and slow living', *Time and Society*, 13 (2/3), 363–82.

Parrinello, J. (2001) 'The technological body in tourism: Research and praxis', *International Sociology*, 16(2), 205–19.

Patke, R.S. (2000) 'Benjamin's arcades project and the postcolonial city', *Diacritics*, 30(4), 2–14.

Peirce, C.M. (1998) 'Harvard lectures on pragmaticism', in N. Houser and C. Kloesel (eds) *The Essential Peirce*, I (Bloomington: Indiana University Press).

Pelé (1977), dir. Francois Reichenbach, Televisa.

Pelé (1977) *Sergio Mendes*, Brazil: Atlantic.

People's Daily (30 August 2012) 'Sebastian Coe hails London 2012 Paralympics', http://english.peopledaily.com.cn/90779/7930055.html, date accessed 8 September 2012.

Peristiany, J. G. (ed.) (1965) *Honour and Shame* (London: Weidenfeld and Nicolson).

Petridis, A. (13 August 2013) 'Olympics closing ceremony music: Big acts, big hits, but no big gasps', *The Guardian*, http://www.guardian.co.uk/sport/2012/aug/13/olympics-closing-ceremony-music-review?intcmp=239, date accessed 13 September 2012.

DOI: 10.1057/9781137336323

Pickel A. (2004) 'Homo nationis: The psychosocial infrastructure of the nation-state order', Annual meeting of the American Sociological Association, San Francisco, CA, http://www.allacademic.com/meta/p109061_index.html, date accessed 21 September 2007.

Plato (1974) *The Republic* (London: Hackett).

Polanyi, K. (1944) *The Great Transformation* (Boston: Beacon Press).

Polanyi, M. (1966) *The Tacit Dimension* (New York: Doubleday).

Pollack, A. (1999) 'Notes on "Here Comes The Sun"', http://www.icce.rug.nl/~soundscapes/DATABASES/AWP/hcts.shtml, date accessed 15 September 2012.

Popovitch, A. (2011) 'Debating Latin American aesthetic theory: Beatriz Sarlo on the autonomy of art', *Bulletin of Latin American Research*, 31(1), 36–50.

Poster, M. (1995) *The Second Media Age* (Cambridge: Polity).

Poster, M. (1997) 'Cyber democracy: Internet and the public sphere', in M. Poster (ed.) *Internet Culture*, New York: Routledge.

Poulter, J. (2009) 'ReMembering the nation: Remembrance days and the nation in Ireland', in D. McCrone and G. McPherson (eds) *National Days* (London: Palgrave Macmillan), 57–72.

Poulter, J. (2013, forthcoming) 'Remembering war, building peace: The role of remembrance of the First World War in the peace process in Northern Ireland', in O. Cetin (ed.) *Cutural Memory and Co-Existence* (International Praxis Conference on Cultural Memory and Coexistence, March 2011, Istanbul: Fatih University).

Powell, A. (1988) 'Like a Rolling Stone: Notions of youth travel and tourism in pop music of the sixties, seventies, and eighties', KAS Papers, http://digitalassets.lib.berkeley.edu/anthpubs/ucb/text/kas067_068-006.pdf, date accessed 5 September 2012.

Pred, A. (1991) 'Spectacular articulations of modernity: The Stockholm exhibition of 1897', *Geograiske Annaler*, 73, 45–84.

Prentice, R. (2004) 'Tourist familiarity and imagery', *Annals of Tourism Research*, 31(4), 931–45.

Prentice, R. and S. Guerin (1998) 'The romantic walker? A case study of users of iconic Scottish landscape', *Scottish Geographical Magazine*, 108(2), 180–91.

Proust, M. (2002) *In Search of Lost Time*, I (London: Vintage).

Radin, M.J. (1996) *Contested Commodities* (Cambridge, MA: Harvard University Press).

DOI: 10.1057/9781137336323

Rafter, N. (2006) *Shots in the Mirror*, 2nd edn. (New York: Oxford University Press).

Ranciére, J. (2011) *The Emancipated Spectator* (London: Verso).

Rees, J. (13 August 2012) 'Olympics closing ceremony: A long goodbye to the Games', BBC News Magazine, http://www.bbc.co.uk/news/magazine-19195421, date accessed 16 September 2012.

Reijders, S. (2011) *Places of the Imagination* (Aldershot: Ashgate).

Reuters (23 November 2001) 'UNICEF denies Pelé corruption reports', http://www.sportbusiness.com/news/142571/unicef-denies-pele-corruption-reports, date accessed 22 September 2012.

Review Graveyard (26 November 2010) 'David Arnold –Interview', http://www.reviewgraveyard.com/00_interviews/10–11–26_david-arnold.html, date accessed 13 September 2012.

Rheingold, H. (2000) *The Virtual Community* (Cambridge, MA: MIT).

Richardson, T. and O.B. Jensen (2004) 'The Europeanisation of spatial planning in Britain: New spatial Ideas for old territories?', ESRC/UACES Study Group on the Europeanisation of British Politics and Policy-Making, Sheffield, 23 April 2004 . Available at: http://aei.pitt.edu/1733/1/richardson.pdf date accessed 4 September 2012.

Ricoeur, P. (1984) *Time and Narrative*, I (New York: Columbia University Press).

Ricoeur, P. (1993) *Oneself as Another* (Chicago: University of Chicago Press).

Ricoeur, P. (1999) 'Memory and forgetting', in R. Kearney and M. Dooley (eds) *Questioning Ethics* (London: Routledge), 5–12.

Ricoeur, P. (2005) *The Course of Recognition* (Cambridge, MA: Harvard University Press).

Ritzer, G. (1999) *Enchanting a Disenchanted World* (Thousand Oaks, CA: Pine Forge Press).

Ritzer, G. and Liska A. (1997) ' "McDisneyization" and "post-tourism": Contemporary perspectives on contemporary tourism', in C. Rojek and J. Urry (eds) *Touring Cultures*, (London and New York: Routledge), 96–112.

Robertson, R. (1992) *Globalization* (London: Sage).

Robins, K (2000) 'Encountering globalisation', in D. Held and A.G. McGrew (eds) *The Global Transformations Reader* (Cambridge: Polity), 195–201.

Roche, M. (1996) 'Mega-events and micro-modernization', in Y. Apostolopoulos, S. Leivadi and A. Yannakis (eds) *The Sociology of Tourism* (London: Routledge), 315–47.

DOI: 10.1057/9781137336323

Roche, M. (2000) *Mega-Events and Modernity* (London: Routledge).

Roche, M. (2002) 'The Olympics and "global citizenship"', *Citizenship Studies*, 6(1), 165–81.

Roche, M. (2006) 'Nations, mega-events and international culture', in G. Delanty and K. Kumar (eds), *The Sage Handbook of Nations and Nationalism* (London: Sage), 260–72.

Rojek, C. (2010) *The Labour of Leisure* (London: Sage).

Rowe, D. and C. Gilmour (2009) 'Global sport: Where Wembley Way meets Bollywood Boulevard', *Continuum*, 23(2), 171–82.

Rumford, C. (2007) 'More than a game: Globalization and the post-Westernization of world cricket', *Global Networks*, 7(2), 202–14.

Sagan, C., F.D. Drake, J. Lomberg, L. Salzman, A. Druyan and T. Ferris (1978) *Murmurs of Earth* (New York: Random House).

Sahlins, M. (1972) *Stone Age Economics* (Chicago: Aldine).

Sahlins, M. (1976) *Culture and Political Reason* (Chicago: University of Chicago Press).

Sahlins, M. (1996) 'The sadness of sweetness: The native anthropology of Western cosmology', *Current Anthropology*, 37(3): 395–415.

Sampson, H. and M. Bloor (2007) 'When Jack gets out of the box: The problems of regulating a global industry', *Sociology*, 41(3), 551–69.

Sánchez Taylor, J. (2000) 'Tourism and "embodied" commodities: Sex tourism in the Caribbean', in S. Clift and S. Carter (eds) *Tourism and Sex* (London and New York: Pinter), 41–53.

Sandywell, B. (2011) *Dictionary of Visual Discourse* (Surrey: Ashgate).

Sarlo, B. (1994) 'In pursuit of the popular imaginary: From sentimentalism to technical skill', *Poetics Today*, 15(4), 569–85.

Sarlo, B. (1999) 'Cultural studies and literary criticism at the crossroads of values', *Journal of Latin American Cultural Studies*, 8, 115–24.

Savelli, A. (2009) 'Tourism in Italian sociological thought and study', in G.M.S. Dann and G. Parrinello (eds) *The Sociology of Tourism* (UK: Emerald), 131–68.

Seaton, A.V. (1999) 'War and thanatotourism: Waterloo, 1815–1914', *Annals of Tourism Research*, 26(1), 130–59.

Said, E. (1978) *Orientalism* (London: Penguin).

Said, E. (1994) *Culture and Imperialism* (London: Vintage).

Sassen, S. (2001) *The Global City* (Princeton, NJ: Princeton University Press).

Sassen, S. (2002) (ed.) *Global Networks, Linked Cities* (London: Routledge).

DOI: 10.1057/9781137336323

Sassen, S. (2006) *Territory, Authority, Rights* (Princeton, NJ: Princeton University Press).

Sattler, J. (15 July 2010) 'ARIA by Villa-Lobos, Bachianas Brasileiras No.5', *Authors Den*, http://www.authorsden.com/visit/viewPoetry. asp?id=281132, date accessed 28 September 2012.

Sawer, P. and C. Duffin (12 August 2012) 'Olympics closing ceremony: Spectacular end to the Games will celebrate 50 years of British pop', *The Telegraph*, http://www.telegraph.co.uk/sport/olympics/9469312/ Olympics-closing-ceremony-spectacular-end-to-the-Games-will-celebrate-50-years-of-British-pop.html, date accessed 12 September 2012.

Schechner, R. (1988) *Performance Theory* (London: Routledge).

Scheler, M. (2003) *Ressentiment* (Wisconsin: Marquette University Press).

Scullion, C. (2 June 2009) 'E3: Pele shows his skills for Academy of Champions', *The Official Nintendo Magazine*, http://www. officialnintendomagazine.co.uk/9043/e3-pele-shows-his-skills-for-academy-of-champions/, date accessed 23 September 2012.

Segun, T. (12 August 2012) 'Pelé surprises London 2012 Closing Ceremony crowd with Rio 2016 handover performance', Inside the Games, http://www.insidethegames.biz/olympics/summer-olympics/2012/18228-pele-surprises-london-2012-closing-ceremony-crowd-with-rio-2016-handover-performance-, date accessed 20 March 2013.

Serres, G. (1995) *Genesis* (Ann Harbour: University of Michigan Press).

Serres, G. and B. Latour (1995) *Conversations on Science, Culture and Time* (Ann Arbor: University of Michigan Press).

Sharp, D. (undated) 'The impact of folkloric tourism on the traditional musical style Coco in Pernambuco, Brazil', Dissertation Intellectual Consortium, University of Texas at Austin, https://webspace. utexas.edu/cherwitz/www/ie/samples/sharp.pdf, date accessed 26 September 2012.

Shaw, L. and S. Dennison (2004) *Popular Cinema in Brazil, 1930–2001* (Manchester: Manchester University Press).

Shaw, L. (1999) The Social History of the Brazilian Samba (Aldershot: Ashgate).

Sheller, M. (2000) *Democracy after Slavery* (London: Macmillan).

Sheller, M. (2003) *Consuming the Caribbean* (New York: Routledge).

DOI: 10.1057/9781137336323

Sheller, M. (2004) 'Demobilizing and remobilizing Caribbean paradise', in M. Sheller and J. Urry (eds) *Tourism Mobilities* (London: Routledge), 13–21.

Sheller, M. and J. Urry (2000) 'City and the car', *International Journal of Urban and Regional Research*, 24(4), 737–57.

Sheller, M. and J. Urry (2004) 'Places to play, places in play', in M. Sheller and J. Urry (eds) *Tourism Mobilities* (London: Routledge), 1–10.

Sheller M and J. Urry (2006) 'The new mobilities paradigm', *Environment and Planning A*, 38(2), 207–26.

Shields, R. (1991) *Places on the Margin* (London: Routledge).

Silk, M. (2001) 'Together we're one? The "place" of the nation in media representations of the 1998 Kuala Lumpur Commonwealth Games', *Sociology of Sport Journal*, 18(3), 277–301.

Simoni, V. (2008) 'Shifting power: The destabilisation of asymmetries in the realm of tourism in Cuba', *Tsantsa*, 13, 89–97.

Simpson, K. (2005) 'Broad horizons? Geographies and pedagogies of the gap year', Unpublished Ph.D. Thesis, University of Newcastle, http://www.ethicalvolunteering.org/downloads/final.PDF, retrieved 3 March 2012

Sinclair, J. (2000) 'More than an old flame: National symbolism and the media in the torch ceremony of the Olympics', *Media International Australia*, 97, 35–46.

Singh, S. (2012) 'Slow travel and Indian culture: Philosophical and practical aspects', in S. Fullagar, K. Markwell and E. Wilson (eds) *Slow Tourism* (Bristol: Channel View), 214–26.

Skidmore, T.E. (1990) 'Racial ideas and social policy in Brazil 1870–1940', in R. Graham (ed.) *The Idea of Race in Latin America* (Austin, TX: University of Texas Press), 7–36.

Slater, D. (2002) 'Making things real: Ethics and order on the Internet', *Theory, Culture & Society*, 19(5/6), 227–45.

Smart, B. (2005) *The Sport Star* (London: Sage).

Smith, R. (2007) *Being Human* (New York: Columbia University Press).

Smith, P. (2008) 'The Balinese Cockfight decoded: Reflections on Geertz, the strong programme and structuralism', *Cultural Sociology*, 2(2), 169–86.

Snopes.com (27 April 2007) 'Because', http://www.snopes.com/music/songs/because.asp, date accessed 15 September 2012.

DOI: 10.1057/9781137336323

Snyder, G. (2012) 'The city and the subculture career: Professional street skateboarding in LA', *Ethnography*, 13(3), 306–29.

Sontag, S. (1990) *On Photography* (New York: Doubleday).

Soper, K. (2008) 'Alternative hedonism, cultural theory and the role of aesthetic revisioning', *Cultural Studies*, 22(5), 567–87.

Spode, H. (2009) 'Tourism research and theory in German-speaking countries', in G.M.S. Dann and G. Parrinello (eds) *The Sociology of Tourism* (UK: Emerald), 65–95.

Spooner, B. (1986) 'Weavers and dealers: Authenticity and Oriental carpets', in A. Appadurai (ed.) *The Social Life of Things* (Cambridge: Cambridge University Press), 195–235.

Stallybrass, P. and A. White (1986) *The Politics and Poetics of Transgression* (Ithaca: Cornell University Press).

Stam, R. (1989) *Subversive Pleasures* (Baltimore: John Hopkins University Press).

The Stage (30 September 2005) 'Devlin the detail – Es Devlin', http://www.thestage.co.uk/features/feature.php/9868/devlin-the-detail-es-devlin, date accessed 13 September 2012.

Steger, M.B. (2008) *The Rise of the Global Imaginary* (Oxford: Oxford University Press).

Stone, G., M. Joseph and M. Jones (2003) 'An exploratory study on the use of sports celebrities in advertising: A content analysis', *Sport Marketing Quarterly*, 12(2), 94–102.

Street, J. (2004) 'Celebrity politicians: Popular culture and political representation', *British Journal of Politics and International Relations*, 6(4), 435–45.

Sutcliffe, T. (13 August 2013) 'London Olympics closing ceremony: Eccentric, bewildering – and shameless good fun', *The Independent*, http://www.independent.co.uk/sport/olympics/london-olympics-2012-closing-ceremony-eccentric-bewildering – and-shameless-good-fun-8037281.html, date accessed 13 September 2012.

Szakolczai, A. (2012) 'Dreams, visions and utopias', in M. Hviid Jacobsen and K. Tester (eds) *Utopia* (Farnham: Ashgate), 47–68.

Szerszynski, B. and J. Urry (2006) 'Visuality, mobility and the cosmopolitan', *British Journal of Sociology*, 57(1), 113–31.

Tanner (ed.) (2003) *The Sociology of Art* (London: Routledge).

Tate, S. (2011) '*Heading South*: Love/sex, necropolitics and decolonial romance', *Small Axe*, 35, 43–58.

DOI: 10.1057/9781137336323

Taylor, C. (2004) *Modern Social Imaginaries* (Durham, NC: Duke University Press).

Theobald, W.F. (1992) 'Fractured fairy tale: The real lives of Princess Caroline and Stephanie', *Mademoisselle*, 68–76.

Theobald, W.F. (1998) 'The meaning, scope and measurement of travel and tourism', in W.F. Theobald (ed.) *Global Tourism*, 2nd edn. (Oxford: Butterworth Heinemann), 3–21.

Theodoraki, E. and L. Todd (2012) 'Brand literacy of the modern Olympic Games and interpretations of ancient ideals', Powerpoint Presentation.

Therborn, G. (1995) 'Routes to/through modernity', in M. Featherstone, S. Lash and R. Robertson (eds) *Global Modernities* (London: Sage), 124–39.

Thompson, J. (1995) *The Media and Modernity* (Cambridge: Polity).

Thompson, P. (2012) 'What is concrete about Ernst Bloch's "concrete utopia"?', in M. Hviid Jacobsen and K. Tester (eds) *Utopia* (Farnham: Ashgate), 33–46.

Thompson-Carr, A. (2012) 'Aoraki/Mt Cook and the Mackenzie basin's transition from wilderness to tourist place', *Journal of Tourism Consumption and Practice*, 4(1), 30–58.

Thrift, N. (1996) 'Inhuman geographies: Landscapes of speed, light and power', in N. Thrift (ed.) *Spatial Formations* (London: Sage), 191–250.

Thrift, N. (2006) 'Re-inventing invention: New tendencies in capitalist commodification', *Economy and Society*, 36(2), 279–306.

Thrift, N. (2007) *Non-Representational Theory* (London: Routledge).

Thrift, N. (2008) 'The material practices of glamour', *Journal of Cultural Economy*, 1(1), 9–23.

Titley, G. (2003) 'Cultivating habitats of meaning: Broadcasting, participation and interculturalism', Irish Communications Review, 9, http://www.icr.dit.ie/volume9/articles/Titley.pdf, date accessed 15 May 2012.

Tomaselli, K.G. (2007) ' "Op die grond": Writing in the san/d, surviving crime', in K.G. Tomaselli (ed.) *Writing in the Sand* (New York: Altamira Press), 39–58.

Tomlinson, A. (1996) 'Olympic spectacle: Opening ceremonies and some paradoxes of globalization', *Media, Culture & Society*, 18(4), 583–602.

Tomlinson, A. (2005) *Sport and Leisure Cultures* (Minneapolis, MN: University of Minnesota Press).

DOI: 10.1057/9781137336323

Tomlinson A. and C. Young (2006) 'Introduction', in A. Tomlinson and C. Yound (eds) *National Identity and Global Sports Events* (New York: SUNY), 1–14.

Topping, A. (27 July 2012) 'Olympics opening ceremony: The view from abroad', *The Guardian*, http://www.guardian.co.uk/sport/2012/jul/27/olympics-opening-ceremony-view-from-abroad, date accessed 9 December 2012.

Touraine, A. (1995) *Critique of Modernity* (Oxford: Blackwell).

Towner, J. (1985) 'The Grand Tour: A key phase in the history of tourism', *Annals of Tourism Research*, 12(3), 293–333.

Trey, G. (1992) 'Communicative ethics in the face of alterity: Habermas, Levinas and the problem of post-conventional universalism', *Praxis International*, 11(4), 412–27.

Tsartas, P. and V. Galani-Moutafi (2009) 'The sociology and anthropology of tourism in Greece', in G.M.S. Dann and G. Parrinello (eds) *The Sociology of Tourism* (UK: Emerald), 299–322.

Tudor, A. (1976) 'Genre and critical methodology', in B. Nichols (ed.) *Blurred Boundaries* (Bloomington, IN: Indiana University Press), 118–26.

Turner, B. (1994) *Orientalism, Postmodernism and Globalism* (London and New York: Routledge).

Turner, B.S. (2006) 'Classical sociology and cosmopolitanism: A critical defense of the social', *The British Journal of Sociology*, 57(1), 133–51.

Turner, V. (1969) *The Ritual Process* (New York: Aldine De Gruyter).

Turner, V. (1974) 'Liminal to liminoid, play flow and ritual: An essay in comparative symbolology', *Rice University Studies*, 50, 53–92.

Turner, R. (2 August 2012) 'Underworld's brief to "frighten people" at the London 2012 opening ceremony', *The Guardian*, http://www.guardian.co.uk/music/2012/aug/02/underworld-london-2012-opening-ceremony?commentpage=2#start-of-comments, date accessed 3 September 2012.

Tzanelli, R. (2004) 'Giving gifts (and then taking them back): Identity, reciprocity and symbolic power in the context of Athens 2004', *The Journal of Cultural Research*, 8(4), 425–46.

Tzanelli, R. (2007a) 'Solitary amnesia as national memory: From Habermas to Luhman', *International Journal of Humanities*, 5(4), 253–60.

Tzanelli, R. ([2007b] 2010) *The Cinematic Tourist* (London: Routledge).

DOI: 10.1057/9781137336323

Tzanelli, R. (2008a) *Nation-Building and Identity in Europe* (Basingstoke: Palgrave Macmillan).

Tzanelli, R. (2008b) 'The nation has two voices: Diforia and performativity in Athens 2004', *European Journal of Cultural Studies*, 11(4), 489–508.

Tzanelli, R. (2010a) 'Mediating Cosmopolitanism: Crafting an allegorical imperative through Beijing 2008', *International Review of Sociology*, 20(2), 215–41.

Tzanelli, R. (2010b) 'The Da Vinci node: Networks of neo-pilgrimage in the European cosmopolis', *International Journal of Humanities*, 8(3), 113–28.

Tzanelli, R. (2011) *Cosmopolitan Memory in Europe's 'Backwaters'* (London and New York: Routledge).

Tzanelli, R. (2012a) 'Domesticating the tourist gaze in Thessaloniki's Prigipos', *Ethnography*, 13(3), 278–305.

Tzanelli, R. (2012b) 'Domesticating sweet sadness: Thessaloniki's *glyká* as a travel narrative', *Cultural Studies—Critical Methodologies*, 12(2), 159–72.

Tzanelli, R. (2013) *Heritage in the Digital Era* (London and New York: Routledge).

Tzanelli, R., M. Yar and M. O'Brien (2005) 'Con me if you can: Exploring crime in the American cinematic imagination', *Theoretical Criminology*, 9(1), 97–117.

Urry, J. (1995) *Consuming Places* (London: Routledge).

Urry, J. (1996) 'Tourism, culture and social inequality', in Y. Apostolopoulos, S. Leivadi and A. Yannakis (eds) *The Sociology of Tourism* (London: Routledge), 115–33.

Urry, J. (2000) *Sociology Beyond Societies* (London: Routledge).

Urry, J. (2003) *Global Complexity* (Cambridge: Polity).

Urry, J. (2004) 'Death in Venice', in M. Sheller and J. Urry (eds) *Tourism Mobilities* (London and New York: Routledge), 205–15.

Urry, J. (2007) *Mobilities* (Cambridge: Polity).

Urry, J. (2008) 'The London Olympics and global competition: On the move', *Twenty First Century Society*, 3(3), 289–93.

Urry, J. (2011) *Climate Change and Society* (Cambridge: Polity).

Urry, J. and J. Larsen (2011) *The Tourist Gaze 3.0* (London: Sage).

Uteng, T.P. and T. Cresswell (2008) *Gendered Mobilities* (Aldershot: Ashgate).

Van Dijk, J. (2006) *The Network Society* (London: Sage).

DOI: 10.1057/9781137336323

Van Gennep, A. (1906) *Rites of Passage* (Chicago, IL: University of Chicago Press).

Vannini, P., J. Hodson and A. Vannini (2009) 'Toward a technography of everyday life', *Cultural Studies—Critical Methodologies*, 9(3), 462–76.

Vardiabasis, N. (2002) *Story of a Word* (Athens: Livani).

Veijola, S. and A. Valtonen (2007) 'The body in tourism industry', in A. Pritchard, N. Morgan, I. Ateljevic and C. Harris (eds) *Tourism and Gender* (Wallingford: CABI), 13–31.

Veijola, S. and E. Jokinen (1994) 'The body in tourism', *Theory and Society*, 11, 125–51.

Veloso, C. (2003) *Tropical Truth* (New York: Alfred A. Knopf).

Vicat-Brown, D. (13 August 2012) 'Kate Moss And Naomi Campbell come under fire for Olympics Closing Ceremony catwalk', *Entertainmentwise*, http://www.entertainmentwise.com/news/84611/ Kate-Moss-And-Naomi-Campbell-Come-Under-Fire-For-Olympics-Closing-Ceremony-Catwalk, date accessed 16 September 2012.

Virilio, P. (2006) *Speed and Politics* (New York and Los Angeles: Semiotext).

Wacquant, L. (2001) 'Whores, slaves and stallions: Languages of exploitation and accommodation among boxers', *Body and Society*, 7(2/3), 181–94.

Wain, M. (1998) *Freud's Answer* (Chicago: Ivan R. Dee).

Walby, S. (2009) *Globalization and Inequalities* (London: Sage).

Wall, D. and M. Yar (2010) 'Intellectual property crime and the Internet', in Y. Jewkes and M. Yar (eds) *Handbook of Internet Crime* (Devon: Willan), 255–72.

Weeks, J. (1977) *Coming Out!!* (London: Quartet).

Wenning, M. (2009) 'The return of rage', *Parrhesia*, 8, 89–99.

White, S. (2003) *The Civic Minimum* (Oxford: Oxford University Press).

Wiegman, R. (1998) 'Race, ethnicity and film', in J. Hill and P.C. Gibson (eds) *The Oxford Guide to Film Studies* (Oxford: Oxford University Press), 158–68.

Wikipedia (undated) 'Here Comes the Sun', http://en.wikipedia.org/ wiki/Here_Comes_the_Sun#cite_ref-0, date accessed 15 September 2012.

Wikipedia (undated) 'Marisa Monte', http://en.wikipedia.org/wiki/ Marisa_Monte#cite_note-0, date accessed 22 September 2012.

Williams, R. (13 August 2012) 'London 2012: This closing ceremony was a raucous pageant of popular culture', *The Guardian*, http://www.

DOI: 10.1057/9781137336323

guardian.co.uk/sport/2012/aug/13/olympic-games-closing-ceremony-culture?newsfeed=true, date accessed 13 September 2012.

Williams, R. (1965–61) *The Long Revolution* (Harmondsworth: Penguin).

Williams, R. (1974) *The Country and the City* (New York: Oxford University Press).

Williams, F. (2002) 'The presence of feminism in the future of welfare', *Economy and Society*, 31(4), 502–19.

Williams, F. (2004) *Rethinking Families* (London: Calouste Gulbenkian Foundation).

Wilson, H. (1996) 'What is an Olympic City? Visions of Sydney 2000', *Media, Culture & Society*, 18(4), 603–18.

Witkin, R. (2005) 'A "new" paradigm for the sociology of aesthetics', in D. Inglis and J. Hughson (eds) *The Sociology of Art* (London: Palgrave), 73–86.

Wolff, J. (1984) *The Social Production of Art* (New York: New York University Press).

Wolff, J. (1987) 'The ideology of autonomous art', in R. Leppert and S. McClary (eds) *Music and Society* (Minneapolis: University of Minnesota Press), 1–12.

Wong, E.F. (1978) *On Visual Media Racism* (New York: Arno).

Woodward, K. (2012) *Sporting Times* (Basingstoke: Palgrave Pivot).

Yar, M. (2000) 'From actor to spectator: Hannah Arendt's "two theories" of political action', *Philosophy and Social Criticism*, 26(2), 1–27.

Yar, M. (2012) 'Virtual utopias and dystopias – the imaginary of the Internet', in M. Hviid Jacobsen and K. Tester (eds) *Utopia* (Farnham: Ashgate), 179–96.

Young, I.M. (1990) *Throwing Like a Girl and Other Essays in Feminist Philosophy and Social Theory* (Bloomington, IN: Indiana University Press).

Zeitlyn, D. (2003) 'Gift economies in the development of open source software: Anthropological reflections', *Research Policy* (special issue: Open Source Software Development), University of Kent at Canterbury, http://lucy.ukc.ac.uk/dz/, date accessed 29 March 2012.

Žižek, S. (1991) *For they Know Not What They Do* (New York: Verso).

Žižek, S. (1999) *The Ticklish Subject* (New York: Verso).

DOI: 10.1057/9781137336323

Index

DOI: 10.1057/9781137336323

DOI: 10.1057/9781137336323

DOI: 10.1057/9781137336323

DOI: 10.1057/9781137336323

DOI: 10.1057/9781137336323

DOI: 10.1057/9781137336323

DOI: 10.1057/9781137336323

DOI: 10.1057/9781137336323

scapes, 2, 34, 84
    See also articulation, artscapes,
        cirtyscapes, memoryscapes
Scheidt, Robert, 105, 113
scholé, 13–15, 63, 89, 112–13, 117
    See (athletic) craft, Europe, heritage,
        modernity, mobilities, Olympic
        Games, travel, working-class
Serota, Nikolas, 73
Sex Pistols, 62, 79
Shakespeare(-an), 37, 46, 72, 84–5
    See also articulation, Britain, heritage,
        land, landscape, mobilities,
        nation-building
Shanghai World Expo, 71
signs, 5, 27, 31, 41–3, 4–9, 64, 66, 69, 83,
        89, 99–100, 105–6, 113, 117, 138
    See also cultural industries, (tourist,
        visual) mobilities, node(-s)
Slumdog Millionaire (2008) 38, 80, 109,
        138
slums, Indian 109, 128
    See also Boyle, Danny, favela(-s),
        Slumdog Millionaire
Smith, Rick, 49
sociology
    of absences, 102
    of art, 126, 136, 139, 148, 153
    of giving, 121
    of tourism, 125–6, 138, 144–5, 148,
        150–1
son, 106
Sorriso, Renato, 105–8, 111, 113, 115–16
    See also articulation, BNegão,
        Brasilidade, Brazil, character(-s),
        genre(-s), nation-building,
        performative synaesthetics, salsa,
        samba, symfonía, synaesthesia,
        Jorge (Seu), (labour, slave)
        mobilities
Spall, Timothy, 85
spectacle, 10, 16, 20, 37, 66, 81, 101–4,
        110, 127, 137, 139, 149
    artistic, 32
    audio-visual, 54
    cinematic, 19

global, 13, 52
labour-intensive, 21
national, 26
Olympic, 5, 12, 25, 28, 39, 48, 62, 87
post-modern, 29, 78
tourist, 45, 81
urban, 29
    See also cityscapes, digitopia,
        (imaginary) city, mega-
        event(-s), modernity, node(-s),
        phantasmagoria
spectator(-s), 12, 40–1, 66, 104, 142,
        153
    emancipated, 12, 82, 144
    external, 45
    Olympic, 48, 115
    See diforía, habitus, (radical,
        social) imaginary, mega-events,
        mobilities, synaesthesia
Spice Girls, 79, 93
Star Wars (1977–2005)
Stratford, 76, 131
style(-s), 32, 69, 91, 103–5, 110
    artistic, 7, 57, 112
    bohemian, 29
    catwalk, 91
    consumption, 12
    cosmopolitan, 109
    dancing, 61
    dominant, 57
    embodied, 96
    musical, 63, 106, 108, 146
    sub-cultural, 61
    tourist, 12
    See also articulation, character,
        genre(-s), performative
        synaesthetics, mobilities,
        modernity, (high) modernism,
        postmodernity, spectacle
Sugababes, 62
symfonía, 81
    See also articulation, cosmopolitan
        aesthetics, cosmopolitanism,
        Enlightenment, Kant, nation-
        building
synaesthesia, 12

DOI: 10.1057/9781137336323

DOI: 10.1057/9781137336323

DOI: 10.1057/9781137336323